Reading STREET

Grade 1

Scott Foresman

On-Level Take-Home Readers

ISBN: 0-328-16896-3

2 3 4 5 6 7 8 9 10 V084 14 13 12 11 10 09 08 07 06

PEARSON Scott Foresman

Editorial Offices: Glenview, Illinois • Parsippany, New Jersey • New York, New York
Sales Offices: Boston, Massachusetts • Duluth, Georgia • Glenview, Illinois
Coppell, Texas • Sacramento, California • Mesa, Arizona

Contents

They Are Sick

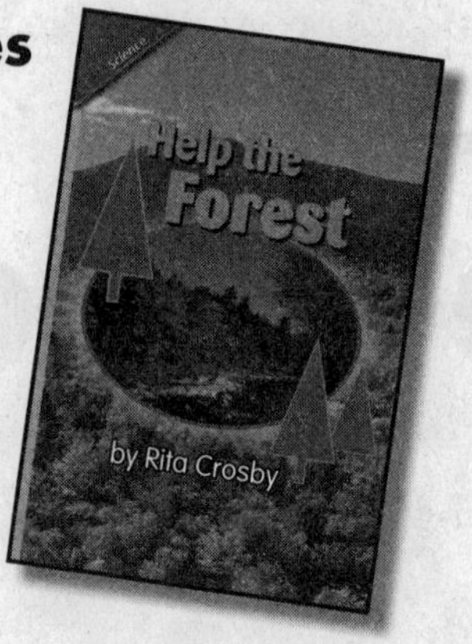

Help the Forest
by Rita Crosby

Life Science
Spring Rose, Winter Bear

Special Days, Special Food
by Juan Lester

Marla's Idea

How to Use the Take-Home Leveled Readers

1. Tear out the pages for each Take-Home Leveled Reader. Make a copy for each child. Be sure to copy both sides of each page.

2. Fold the pages in half to make a booklet.

3. Staple the pages on the left-hand side.

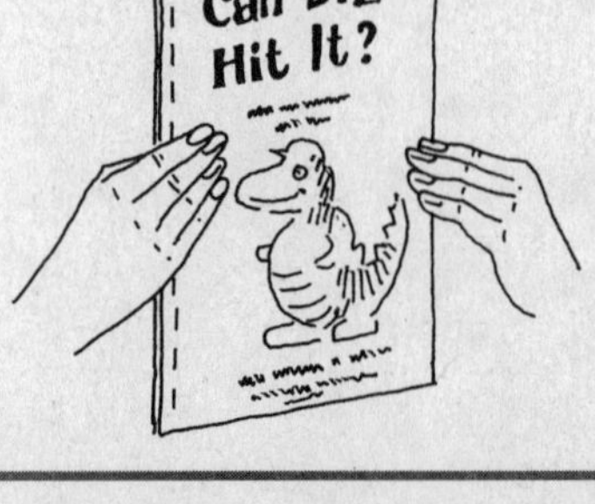

4. Share the Take-Home Leveled Readers with children. Suggest they read these with family members.

Suggested levels for Guided Reading, DRA™, Lexile®, and Reading Recovery™ are provided in the Pearson Scott Foresman Leveling Guide.

Genre	Comprehension Skills and Strategy
Realistic fiction	• Character • Main Idea • Monitor and Fix Up

Scott Foresman Reading Street 1.1.1

PEARSON
Scott Foresman
scottforesman.com

ISBN 0-328-13143-1
9 780328 131433 90000

Mack the Cat

by Ann Rossi

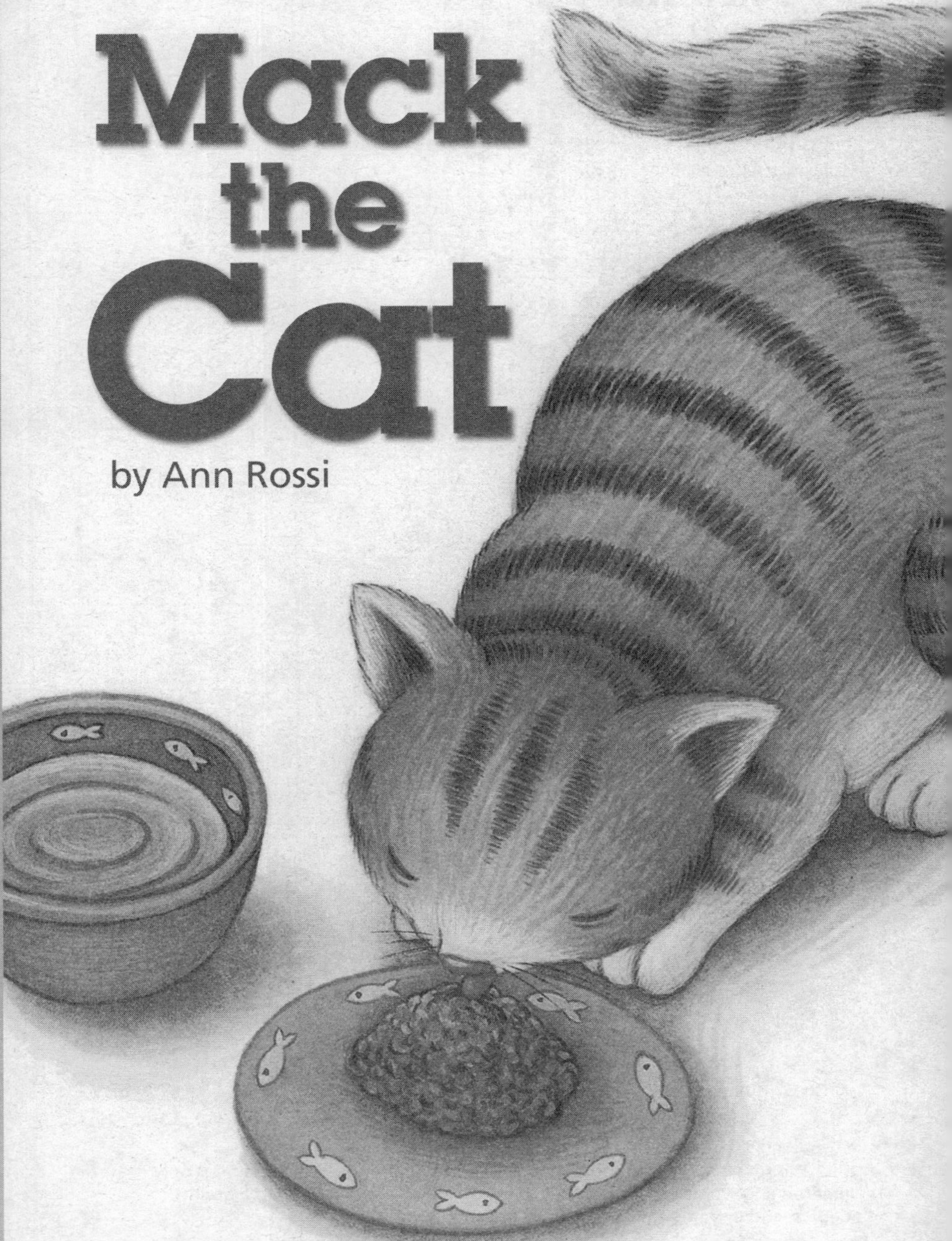

illustrated by Chi Chung

Vocabulary

in

on

way

Word count: 59

Note: The total word count includes words in the running text and headings only. Numerals and words in chapter titles, captions, labels, diagrams, charts, graphs, sidebars, and extra features are not included.

Think and Share

Read Together

1. What did Zack do to care for Mack? Draw the web on your own paper. Point to the circles as you tell your answers.

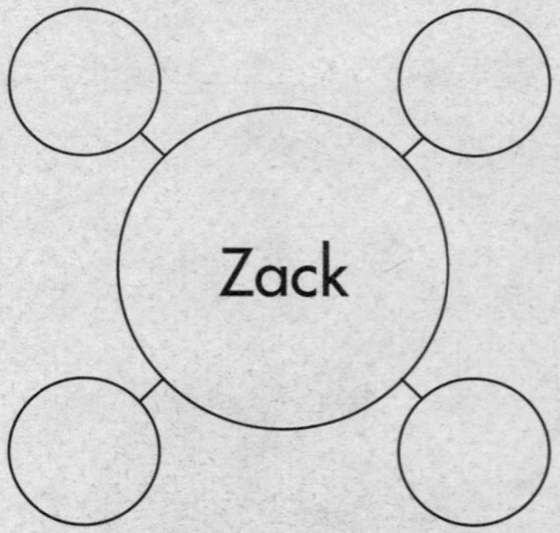

2. Find the place in the book where Mack takes a nap. Where is he when he takes a nap?

3. What sounds do the names Mack and Zack both have?

4. How do the pictures show that Mack likes Zack?

I will make something of my own, she thought. I like bubbles. I like things that are sweet. I will make bubbles you can eat. I will reuse this piece of wire for the wand.

Marla thought about what she might need. She made a list and gave it to her mother. Her mother got everything on the list.

Then Marla measured and mixed. She sifted and stirred. She put in sugar and syrup and other sweet things.

Then, at last, the mixture was done. It was time to carry it into the yard and test it out.

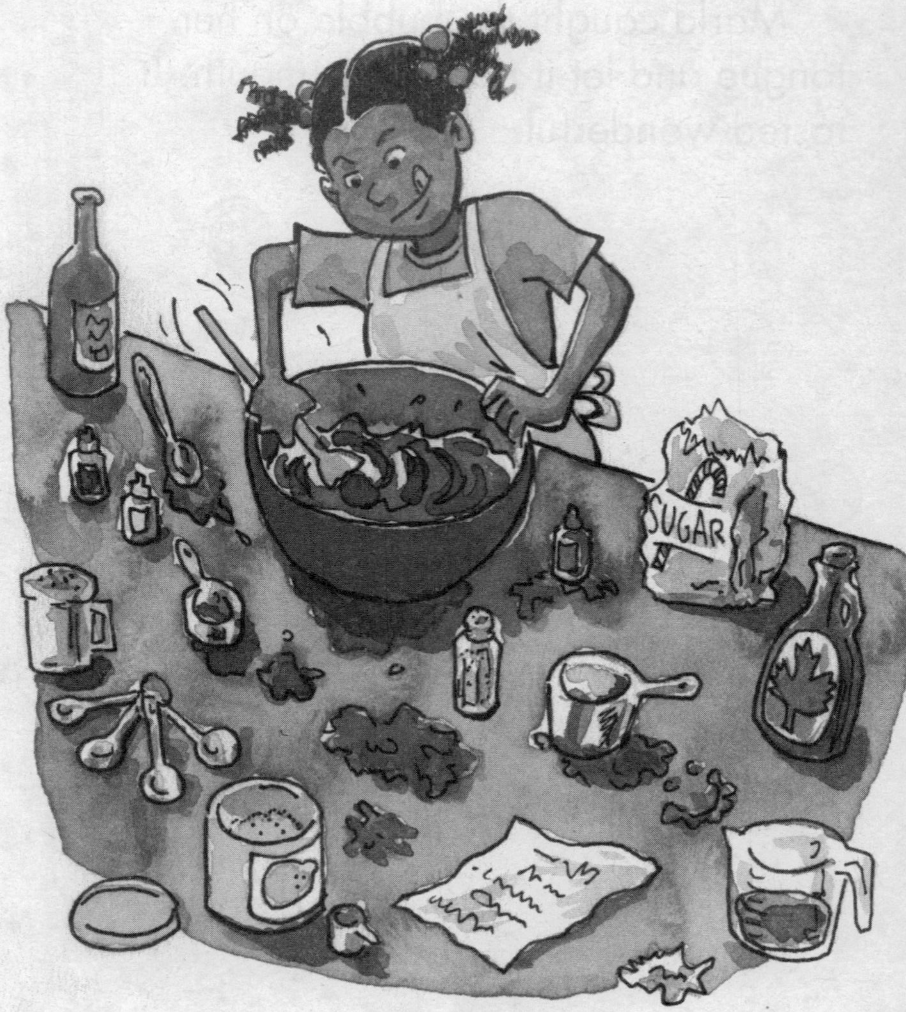

Marla took the wire she had brought from her brothers' room. She made it into a bubble wand. She stuck the bubble wand into the mixture.

Marla blew into the wand. A perfect bubble flew in the air.

Marla caught the bubble on her tongue and let it pop in her mouth. It tasted wonderful.

"I have lots of good ideas," Marla said. "Please let me help."

"You need to find something else to do," answered Mike. "Look, you can have that piece of wire. Just go away and let us do our work."

Poor Marla. She was very unhappy. She almost started to cry. Instead, she got an idea.

"We don't know yet. Please go away so we can think," said her brother Mike.

"I can help you," Marla replied.

"No thank you," said her other brother Dan. "You are not old enough. You are just a little kid and your poor ideas will mess things up."

Marla called her friends Jake and Lucy. They came over to her house.

They blew bubbles and let them land in their mouths. They danced around catching them, laughing and making noise.

Dan and Mike came outside to see what was going on.

"You are not supposed to eat bubbles!" Dan said. "They will make you sick!"

"Not these," said Marla. "I made them special. Try them."

Marla blew a bubble at her brothers. Dan ate one. Mike ate one. Then they ate some more.

Marla was bored. She went to her big brothers' room to see if they wanted to play with her.

"You can't come in," they said. "We are trying to make something for the science fair at our school."

"What will you invent?" Marla asked.

Every effort has been made to secure permission and provide appropriate credit for photographic material. The publisher deeply regrets any omission and pledges to correct errors called to its attention in subsequent editions.

Unless otherwise acknowledged, all photographs are the property of Scott Foresman, a division of Pearson Education.

ISBN: 0-328-13230-6

2 3 4 5 6 7 8 9 10 V010 14 13 12 11 10 09 08 07 06 05

"Marla, you are most amazing," said Dan.

"These are yummy! You have given me an idea for the science fair. We can make a machine that blows different flavors of your bubbles at the same time," Mike said.

"Yes," said Dan. "Will you help us make it?"

Marla smiled. She said, "I think that is a great idea!"

A Cool Kid Invention

Read Together

Have you ever eaten a Popsicle™? Did you know that a kid invented them? It's true. Frank Epperson invented Popsicles when he was just 11 years old.

Frank liked to mix together different flavors of soda. He wanted to know how they would taste if they were frozen. So, one very cold day, he mixed some sodas together in a glass. He put the glass outside. The next morning the drink was frozen solid. The wooden stirring stick was still in it. He pulled the stick out. Out came the frozen drink. It tasted great, and that was the beginning of the Popsicle.

Marla's Idea

by Rosa Lester illustrated by Sean O'Neill

PEARSON
Scott Foresman

Editorial Offices: Glenview, Illinois • Parsippany, New Jersey • New York, New York
Sales Offices: Needham, Massachusetts • Duluth, Georgia • Glenview, Illinois
Coppell, Texas • Ontario, California • Mesa, Arizona

Vocabulary

answered
brothers
carry
different
poor

Word count: 443

Note: The total word count includes words in the running text and headings only. Numerals and words in chapter titles, captions, labels, diagrams, charts, graphs, sidebars, and extra features are not included.

Think and Share

Read Together

1. What might be another good title for this book?
2. What questions would you ask Marla about her invention? Write them in a chart like this. Let friends write answers.

Question	Answer

3. Make word cards for these vocabulary words: *answered, brothers, carry, different, poor.* Turn the cards face down. Use them to tell a story to a partner. Start a story, such as *One day, a little girl was walking down the street.* Turn over a card. Use the word in a sentence. Use the rest of the cards until the story is told.
4. Have you ever had an idea for an invention? What was it?

Suggested levels for Guided Reading, DRA,™ Lexile,® and Reading Recovery™ are provided in the Pearson Scott Foresman Leveling Guide.

Genre	Comprehension Skills and Strategy
Realistic fiction	• Theme • Sequence • Ask Questions

Scott Foresman Reading Street 1.5.6

ISBN 0-328-13230-6

PEARSON Scott Foresman

scottforesman.com

Marla's Idea

by Rosa Lester

illustrated by Sean O'Neill

Written note

Drum and smoke signals could send messages quickly and far away. But the messages couldn't be very long.

People could carry longer messages from place to place. Once people could write, they began to send written notes.

Later, people started sending messages in letters through the mail.

Before there were trains or cars, people used horses to take mail from one place to another.

Mail

Even though people ran or rode fast horses, the mail took a long time to get from one place to the next.

Pigeons are small, fast birds that can be taught to fly from one place to another. People would strap a small note to a pigeon's leg. The pigeon would then fly with the note.

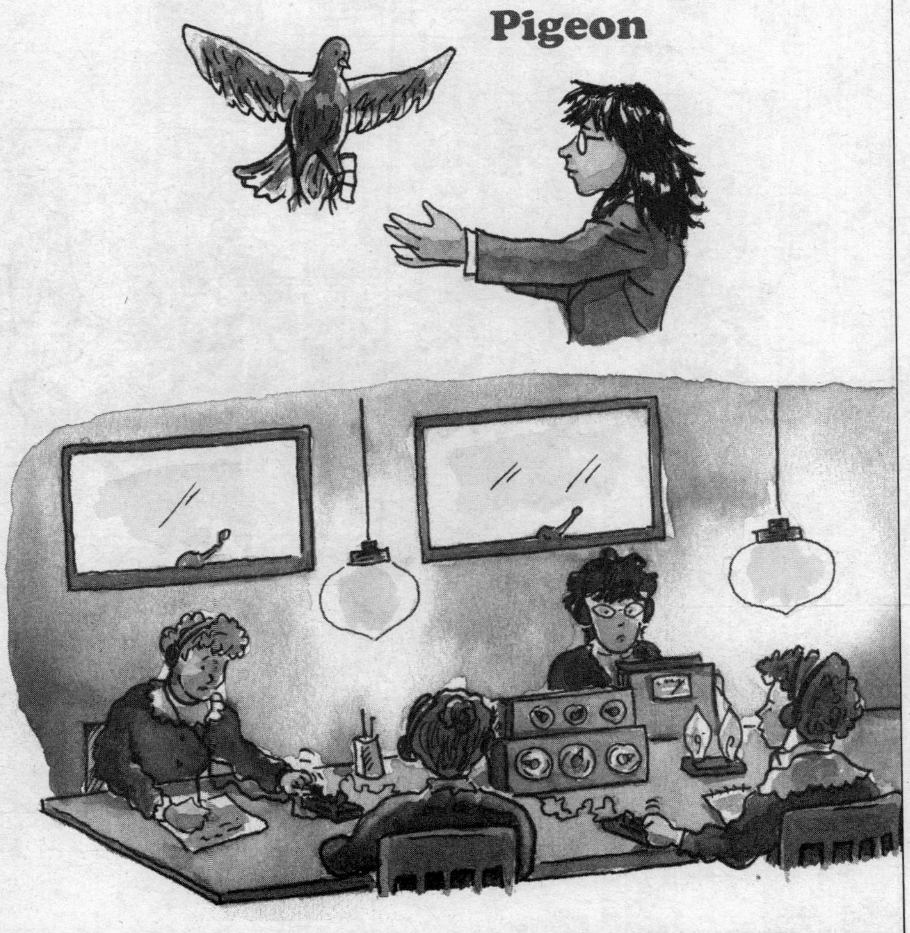

Some groups of people used drums to send messages. The sounds the drums made could be heard far away.

People played drums to tell others when hunts or parties were going to happen.

Smoke

Some people used smoke to send messages. They would wave blankets over a smoky fire. Puffs of smoke would rise into the air. Different numbers of smoke puffs meant different things. For example, one puff of smoke might mean danger!

People far away saw the smoke and could read the messages.

In 1844, the first telegraph message was sent by a man named Samuel Morse. This was a new way to communicate.

Using electricity, Morse made a machine that sent beeps from one place to another. The beeps stood for the alphabet. For example, one fast beep and one slow beep meant the letter A.

Telegraph

Telephone

Then, a man named Alexander Bell tried to make a different machine. He knew a lot about science. He thought he could send spoken words, not just beeps, through electric wires.

In 1876, Bell built the first telephone, a machine that sent spoken words by electricity. Now people could talk to each other right away!

If you want to talk with someone who is far away, you can call them on the telephone. But what did people do before there were telephones?

People have always communicated with others who were far away. They found many ways to do that. Let's learn about some of the early ways.

Every effort has been made to secure permission and provide appropriate credit for photographic material. The publisher deeply regrets any omission and pledges to correct errors called to its attention in subsequent editions.

ISBN: 0-328-13227-6

2 3 4 5 6 7 8 9 10 V010 14 13 12 11 10 09 08 07 06 05

Telephones have changed a lot since Bell's first phone. Now, there are different kinds of telephones. What kinds of phones can you see in the picture?

Computer

Using the telephone is a fast way to communicate to people far away. What about a computer? A lot of people send messages to each other through their computers. Have you ever done that?

Over the years, people have found many ways to communicate over great distances. Soon, we may learn even more.

The Story of Communication

by
Betty Bacon

illustrated by
Sean O'Neill

PEARSON Scott Foresman

Editorial Offices: Glenview, Illinois • Parsippany, New Jersey • New York, New York
Sales Offices: Needham, Massachusetts • Duluth, Georgia • Glenview, Illinois
Coppell, Texas • Ontario, California • Mesa, Arizona

Vocabulary

built

early

learn

science

through

Word count: 444

Note: The total word count includes words in the running text and headings only. Numerals and words in chapter titles, captions, labels, diagrams, charts, graphs, sidebars, and extra features are not included.

Think and Share

Read Together

1. Why do you think people have come up with so many different ways to communicate over long distances?
2. Did any information in this book confuse you? Go back and reread. Use the illustrations on the page to review the ideas. Make a list of important facts on the page. Use a chart like the one below to help you.

Page	Important Facts

3. Go back through the book and find the words *built*, *early*, *learn*, *science*, and *through*. Write a sentence for each word.
4. What do you think future phones will look and act like? Imagine one future phone and draw a picture of it. Present it to the class.

Suggested levels for Guided Reading, DRA,™ Lexile,® and Reading Recovery™ are provided in the Pearson Scott Foresman Leveling Guide.

Social Studies

Genre	Comprehension Skills and Strategy	Text Features
Expository nonfiction	• Draw Conclusions • Compare and Contrast • Monitor and Fix Up	• Labels

Scott Foresman Reading Street 1.5.5

PEARSON
Scott Foresman

scottforesman.com

ISBN 0-328-13227-6
9 780328 132270 90000

Social Studies

The Story of Communication

by Betty Bacon

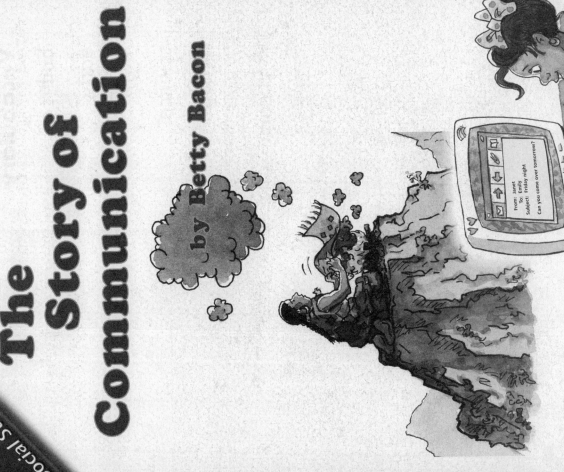

illustrated by Sean O'Neill

Inclined planes make it easier to move things up or down.

The road in this picture is an inclined plane. The slide on your playground is also an inclined plane.

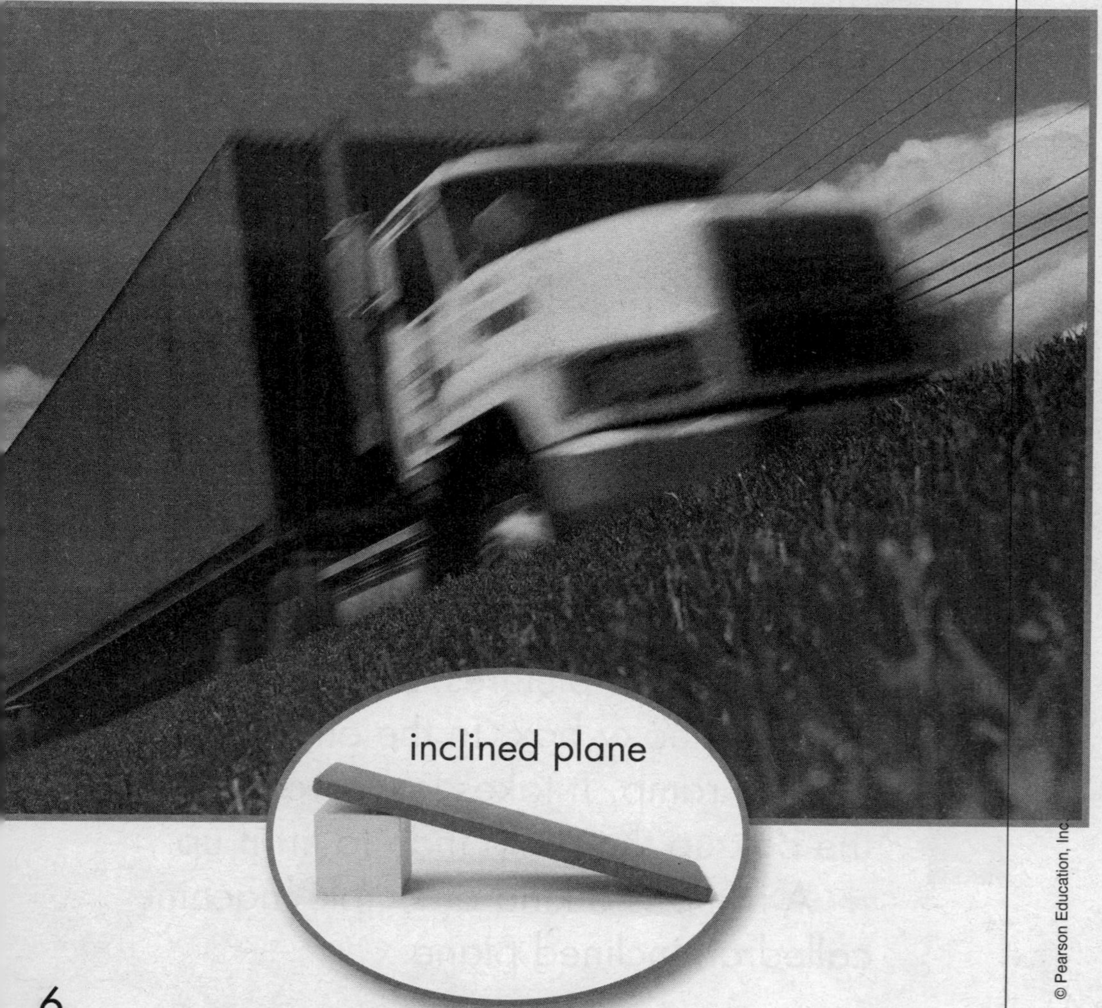

A wedge is another kind of simple machine.

An ax is a kind of wedge. It goes into the wood and splits it apart.

A screw is also a simple machine. The lid of a jar and the bottom of a light bulb are both kinds of screws.

Screws make it easier to put things together. Think about the lid on a jar. As you turn the lid, it screws down onto the jar, closing it tightly.

Look at the pictures. In one, a boy is lifting a heavy box. In the other, a boy is using a ramp. It takes less force to slide the box up the ramp than to lift it up.

A ramp is a kind of simple machine called an inclined plane.

There are six kinds of simple machines. Have you ever seen any of these machines before?

To understand how simple machines work, you need to know about force. Force makes things move. You use force when you push against something or pull something.

In the pictures above, you see levers. A lever is a simple machine for pushing things up. When you push down on one end of the lever, the other end goes up.

Did you know that a seesaw is also a lever?

A pulley is a simple machine used for lifting things.

When you pull on one end of a pulley's rope or chain, whatever is on the other end goes up.

The child in the picture above is using a pulley to hoist the flag.

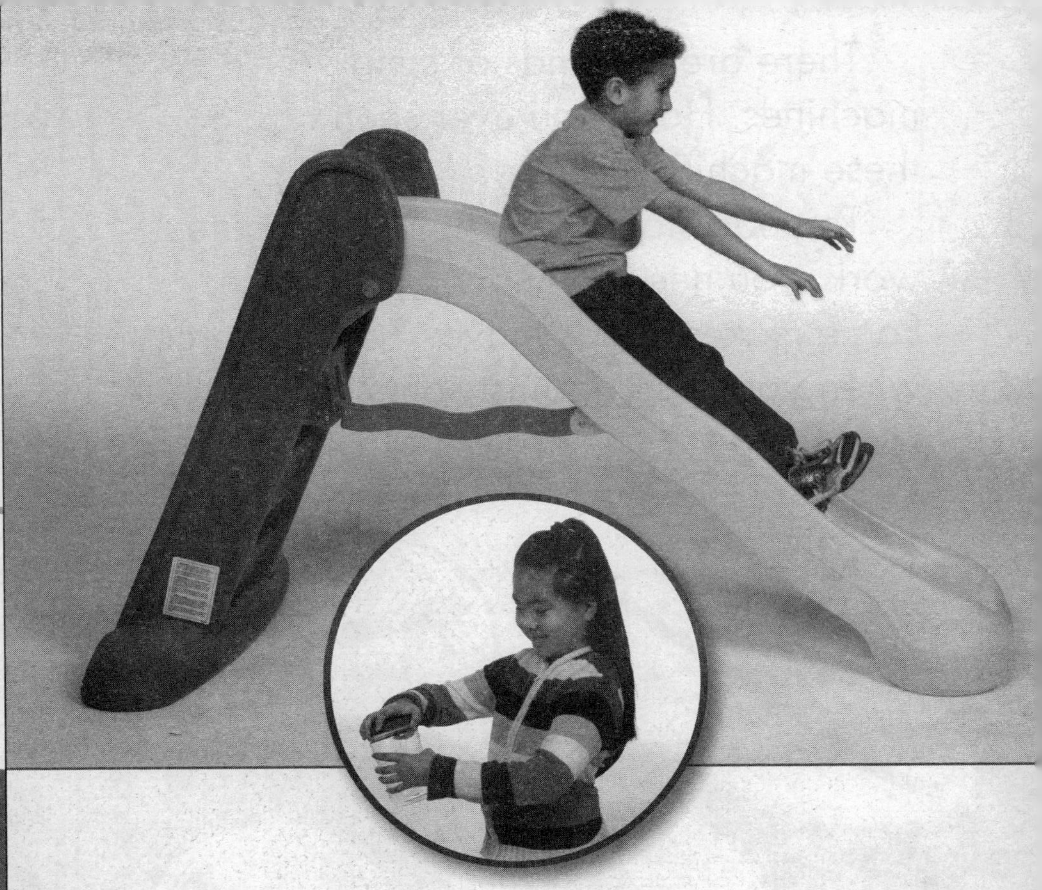

When someone says the word *machine,* do you think of a slide or a jar lid? These objects really are machines. They are called simple machines. Simple machines help you do work with less force.

Photo locators denoted as follows: Top (T), Center (C), Bottom (B), Left (L), Right (R), Background (Bkgd)

1 © Howard Sokol/Stone/Getty Images; 7 (R) © Howard Sokol/Stone/Getty Images.
12 ©Dorling Kindersley Media Library

ISBN: 0-328-13224-9

2 3 4 5 6 7 8 9 10 V010 14 13 12 11 10 09 08 07 06 05

The last simple machine is a wheel and axle. The axle is a kind of rod, or bar, that goes through the wheel. Together, they turn and help things move.

Cars, bikes, and wagons all use wheels and axles.

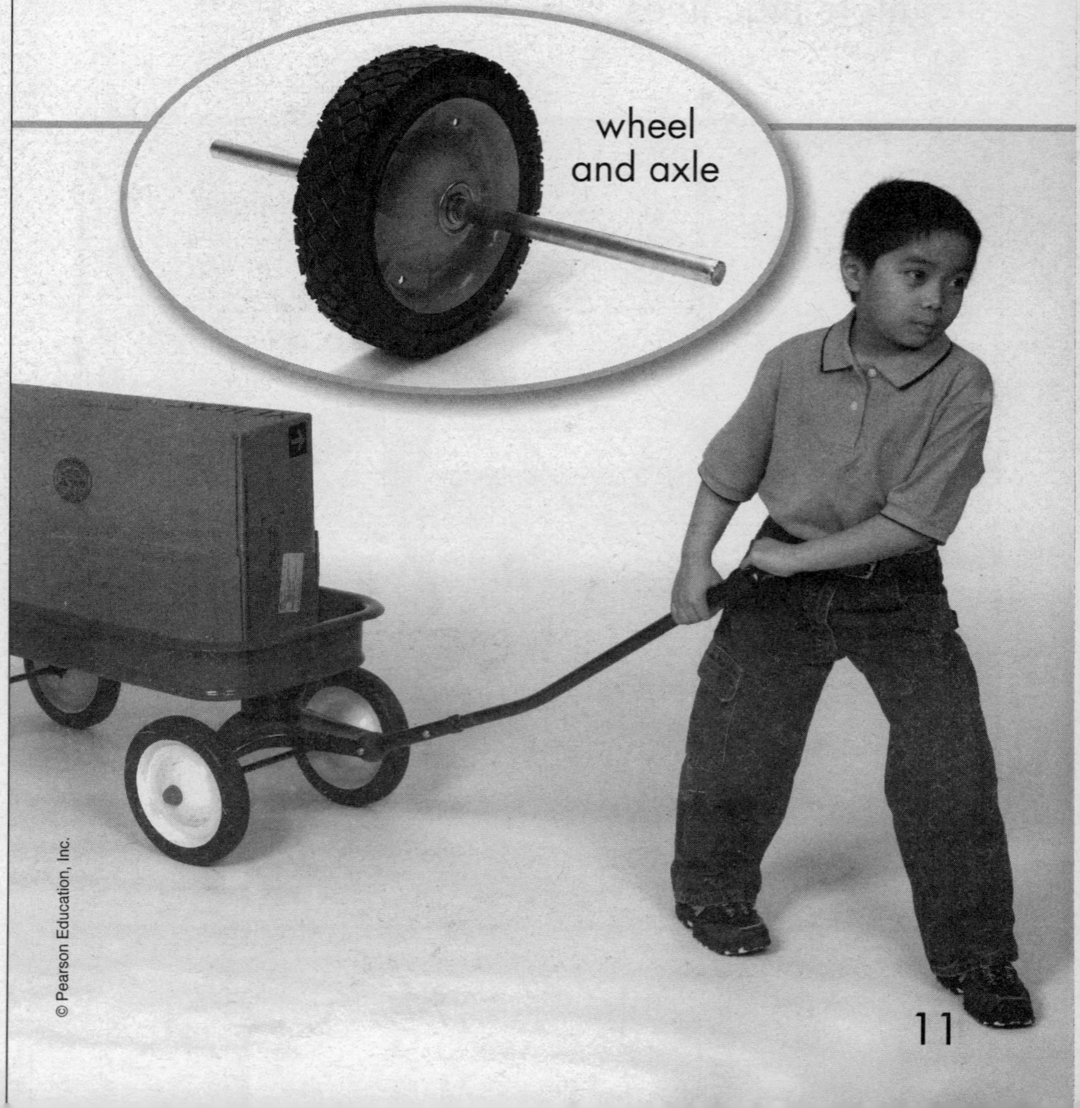

Simple machines make it easier to do work. They let you move an object with less force.

People have used simple machines since long ago. We still use them today. All kinds of workers are glad to have simple machines.

Simple Machines at Work

by Mary Katherine Tate

PEARSON
Scott Foresman

Editorial Offices: Glenview, Illinois • Parsippany, New Jersey • New York, New York
Sales Offices: Needham, Massachusetts • Duluth, Georgia • Glenview, Illinois
Coppell, Texas • Ontario, California • Mesa, Arizona

Vocabulary

against
goes
heavy
kinds
today

Word count: 399

Note: The total word count includes words in the running text and headings only. Numerals and words in chapter titles, captions, labels, diagrams, charts, graphs, sidebars, and extra features are not included.

Think and Share

Read Together

1. What is the main idea of this book?
2. Copy and complete the web. Use the web to write two or three sentences that tell what the book is about.

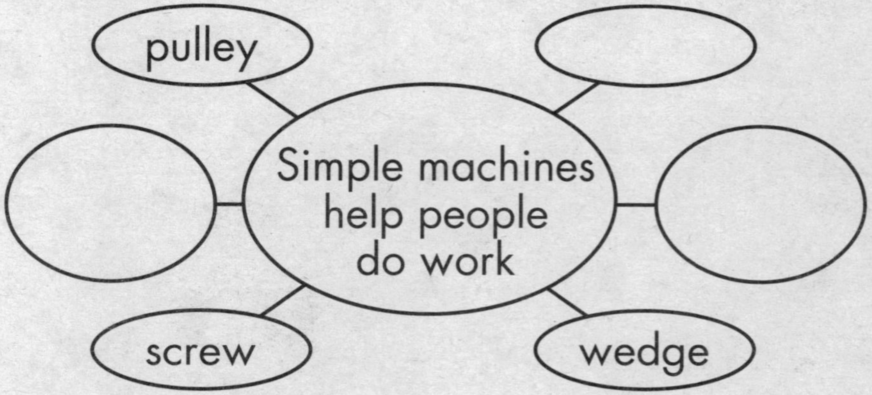

3. Draw a picture of a simple machine. Label your picture. Write a sentence to go with it that describes how it works. If possible, use some of these words: *against, goes, heavy*.
4. Look at pages 5–6. If this were a chapter in the book, what would be a good title for the chapter?

Suggested levels for Guided Reading, DRA, Lexile,® and Reading Recovery™ are provided in the Pearson Scott Foresman Leveling Guide.

Science

Genre	Comprehension Skills and Strategy	Text Features
Expository nonfiction	• Main Idea • Compare and Contrast • Summarize	• Labels

Scott Foresman Reading Street 1.5.4

PEARSON
Scott Foresman

scottforesman.com

ISBN 0-328-13224-9
9 780328 132249 90000

Science

Physical Science

Simple Machines at Work

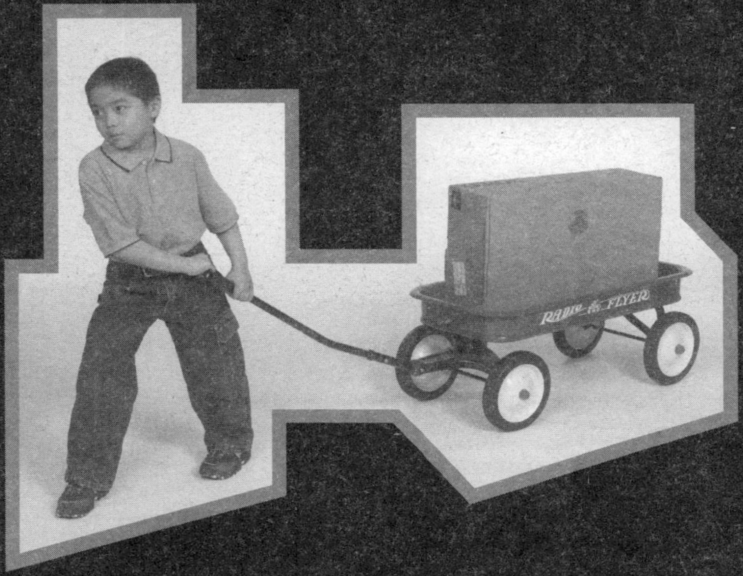

by Mary Katherine Tate

Oak trees can live for hundreds of years. How old do you think this tree is now?

An oak tree reaches high into the air. Some oak trees are more than one hundred feet tall!

One oak tree in Maryland grew to be ninety-six feet tall. Its trunk was thirty-two feet around! It would fill up your bedroom. That tree lived to be 460 years old. Then in 2002, it fell down in a big storm.

This oak tree in Maryland lived 460 years.

There are many large oak trees. It is hard to say which tree is the tallest. It is also hard to say which tree is the oldest. None of these trees live forever. But some live for a very long time!

This oak tree in Virginia is five hundred years old!

Oak trees start out small. But then they keep growing and growing!

Water from the soil and light from the sun help the acorn to sprout and grow. Soon another oak tree stretches to the sky.

How does an oak tree begin its life?

An oak tree starts as an acorn. An acorn is a nut with a seed inside. When the seed is planted in the ground, the oak tree starts to grow.

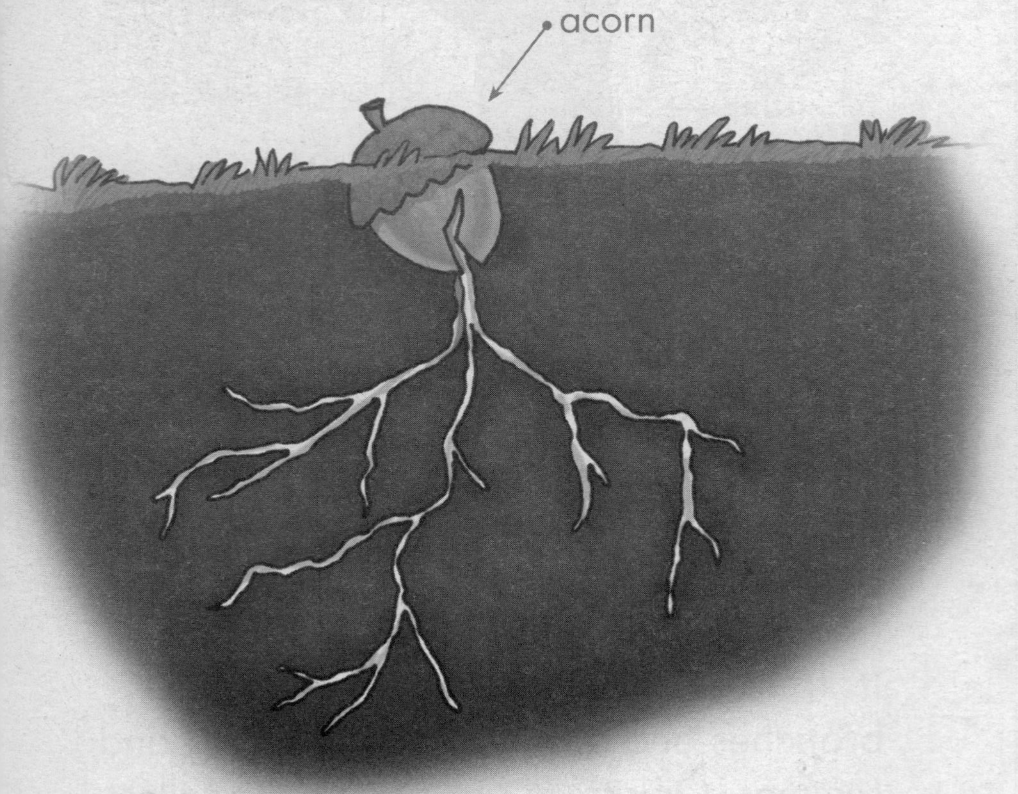

In the fall, oak leaves turn many beautiful colors. Then the oak trees drop their leaves.

Have you ever raked leaves in the fall? You could look for oak leaves when you are raking!

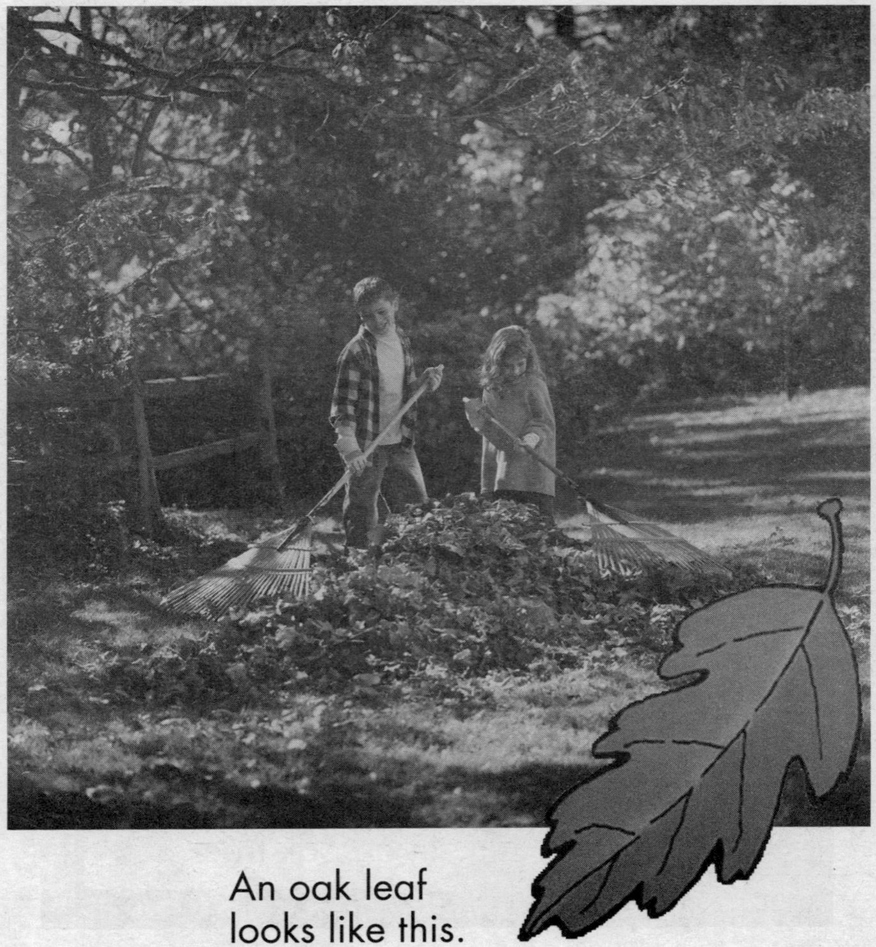

An oak leaf looks like this.

Oak trees are home to many animals. Birds like to make nests in oak trees. Squirrels live in oak trees too.

Other animals, instead of living there, use oak trees for food. Deer, bears, and squirrels all eat acorns from oak trees.

This owl made a home for her family in an oak tree.

This is an oak tree. Have you ever seen one?

An oak tree has gray or black bark. Its trunk is large. An oak tree has thin branches and green leaves in spring and summer. Oak trees are among the tallest trees around.

Every effort has been made to secure permission and provide appropriate credit for photographic material. The publisher deeply regrets any omission and pledges to correct errors called to its attention in subsequent editions.

Unless otherwise acknowledged, all photographs are the property of Scott Foresman, a division of Pearson Education.

Photo locators denoted as follows: Top (T), Center (C), Bottom (B), Left (L), Right (R), Background (Bkgd)

Cover ©Lee Snider/Photo Images/CORBIS; 1 ©Roger Wilmshurst; Frank Lane Picture Agency/CORBIS; 7 ©Lee Snider/Photo Images/CORBIS; 8 ©Carl & Ann Purcell/CORBIS; 9 ©Richard Hutchings/CORBIS; 10 ©Roger Wilmshurst; Frank Lane Picture Agency/CORBIS; 11 ©Massimo Listri/CORBIS; 12 ©Philip Gould/CORBIS

ISBN: 0-328-13221-7

2 3 4 5 6 7 8 9 10 V010 14 13 12 11 10 09 08 07 06 05

People also like oak trees. Oak trees give shade from the sun, and they are beautiful to look at.

Wood from an oak tree is good for making chairs and other furniture.

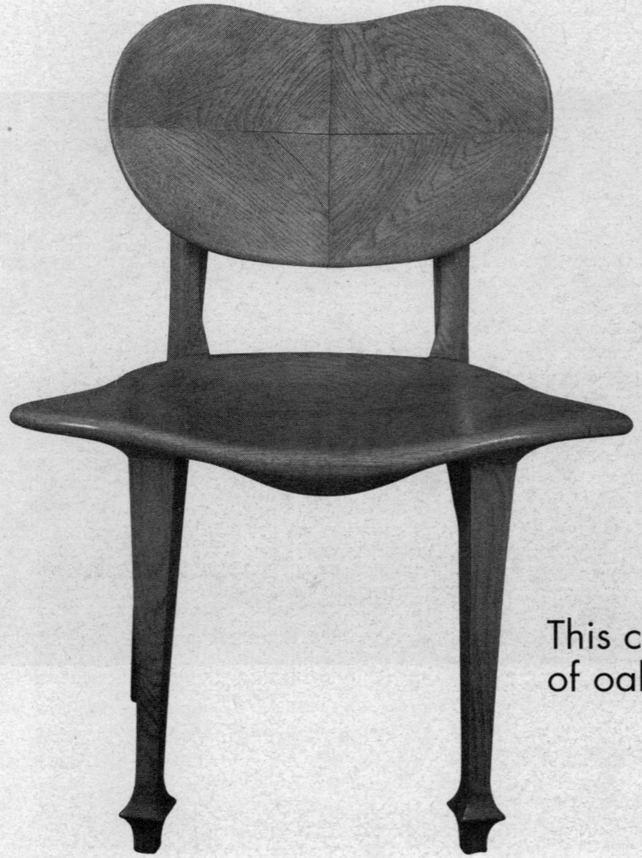

This chair is made of oak wood.

The next time you are out walking, look for an oak tree.

If you like oak trees, you could try planting and growing one of your own. All you need is one acorn!

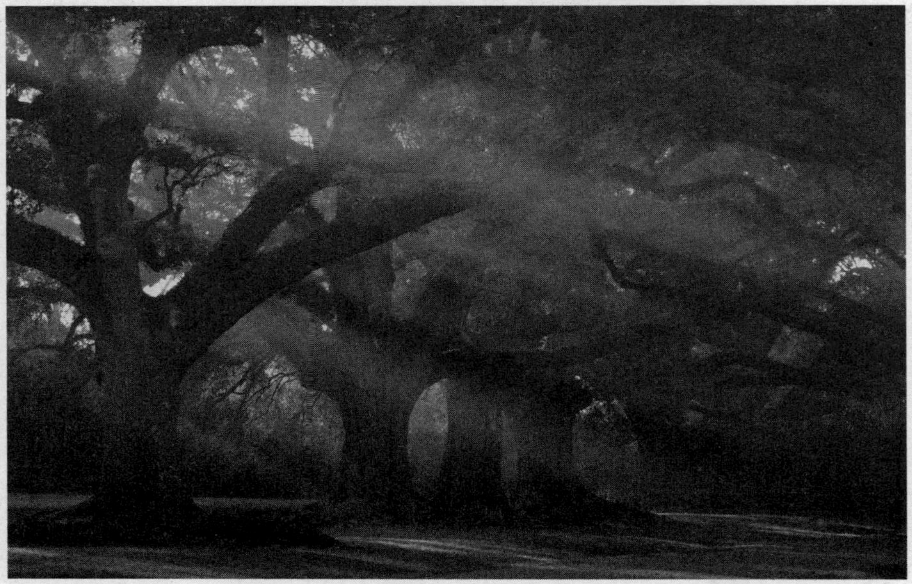

Oak Trees

by Kristin Cashore
illustrated by Donna Catanese

PEARSON Scott Foresman

Editorial Offices: Glenview, Illinois • Parsippany, New Jersey • New York, New York
Sales Offices: Needham, Massachusetts • Duluth, Georgia • Glenview, Illinois
Coppell, Texas • Ontario, California • Mesa, Arizona

Vocabulary

among

another

instead

none

Word count: 375

Note: The total word count includes words in the running text and headings only. Numerals and words in chapter titles, captions, labels, diagrams, charts, graphs, sidebars, and extra features are not included.

Think and Share

Read Together

1. Compare the way animals use oak trees with the way people use oak trees. Use a chart like the one below to give examples.

How Animals Use Oak Trees	How People Use Oak Trees

2. What things help an oak tree to grow? Read the book again if you need help remembering.

3. On a sheet of paper, write all the words from this book that end with *–ing*. Write each base word.

4. Look at the picture on page 5. Then, look at the picture on page 6. How has the tree changed?

Suggested levels for Guided Reading, DRA,™ Lexile,® and Reading Recovery™ are provided in the Pearson Scott Foresman Leveling Guide.

Science

Genre	Comprehension Skills and Strategy	Text Features
Expository nonfiction	• Compare and Contrast • Draw Conclusions • Monitor and Fix Up	• Captions • Diagram • Labels

Scott Foresman Reading Street 1.5.3

PEARSON Scott Foresman

scottforesman.com

ISBN 0-328-13221-7

9 780328 132218 90000

Science

Earth Science

Oak Trees

by Kristin Cashore
illustrated by Donna Catanese

"Well," said Sally, "a puppy raiser gets a new puppy and keeps it at home. A puppy raiser gives the puppy lots of love so that it will know how to love people."

"Hmm," said her mother. "You are good at giving love. You could teach a puppy that."

"There's more," said Sally. "A puppy raiser must help the puppy understand things like *sit* and *stay*. A guide dog should always obey."

"Hmm," said her mother. "You are good at doing what you are told. You could teach a puppy that."

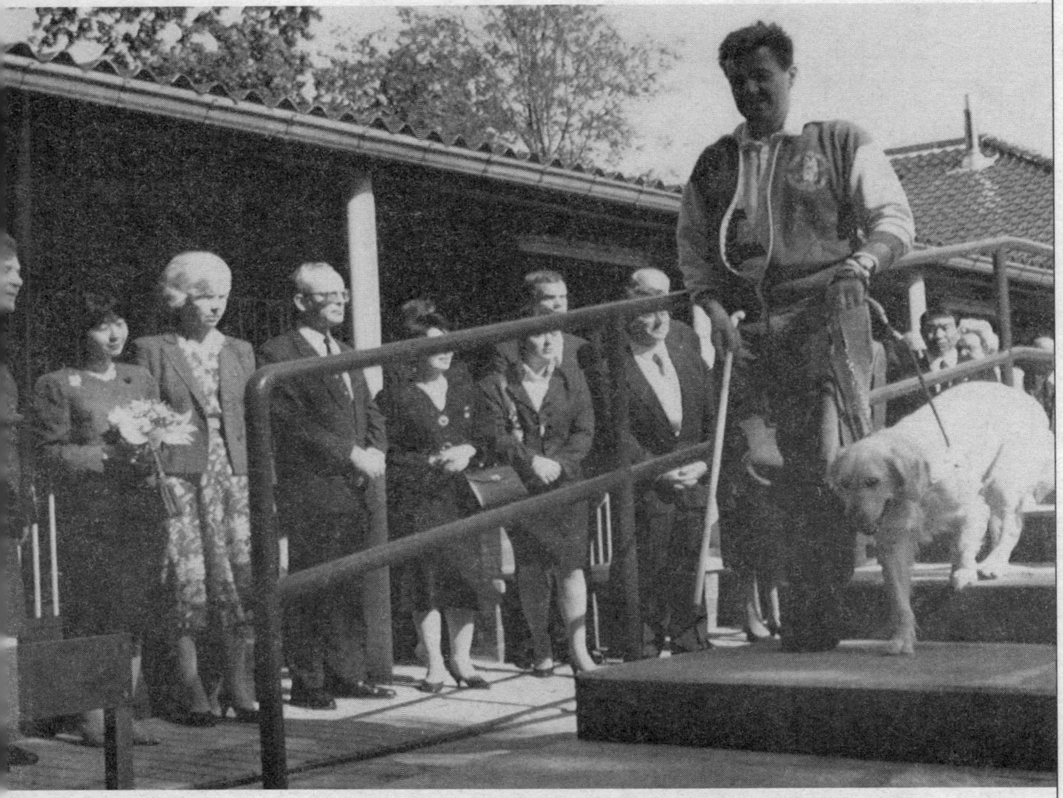

"A guide dog will go to many places with its owner. It should learn to be around many people," Sally said. "A puppy raiser will take the puppy to meet new people."

"Hmm," said her mother. "You are good at meeting new people. You could teach a puppy that."

Sally ran in the door. She had heard about people who raise guide dogs. Sally loves helping people. She loves dogs too.

"Mom," said Sally, "I want to raise a puppy to be a guide dog."

"Hmm," said Sally's mother. "Tell me what you know about it."

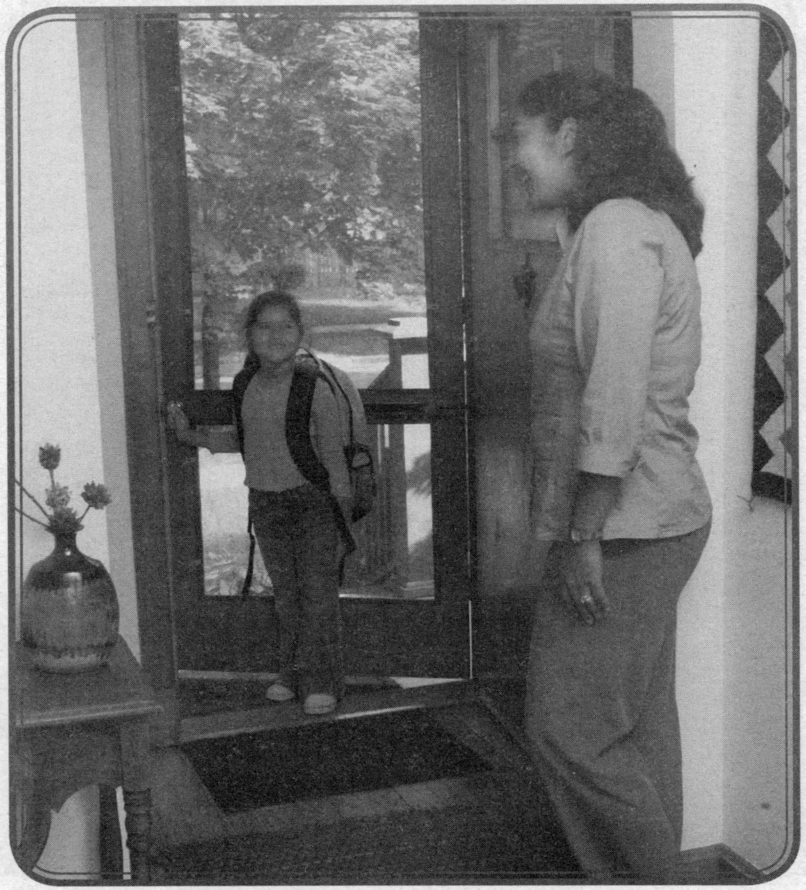

Before dogs can become guide dogs, they need to learn how to behave. They start learning when they are puppies. People who teach these puppies and take care of them are called puppy raisers.

You will read about a girl who wants to be a puppy raiser.

"A guide dog will help its owner travel," said Sally. "The puppy must get used to cars, trains, and buses."

"Hmm," said her mother. "You are good at traveling. You could teach a puppy that."

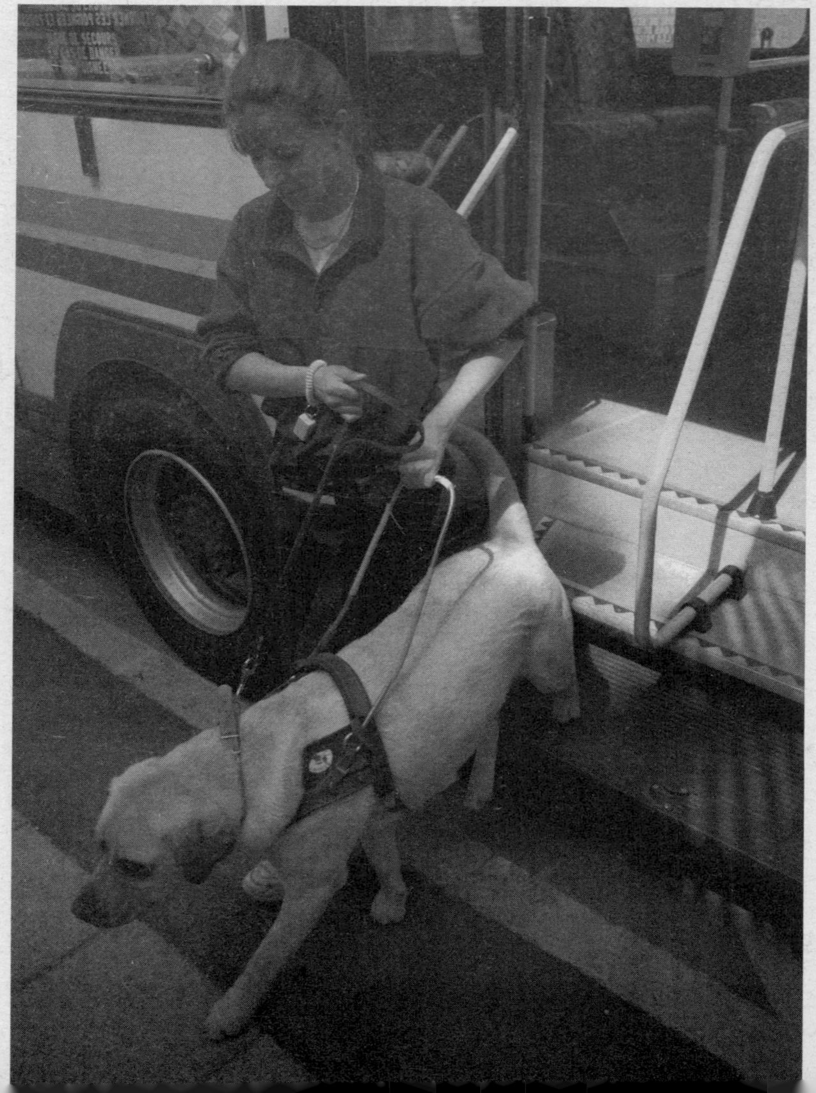

Sally's mother thought for a moment. Then she said, "What happens when the puppy gets older?"

"When the puppy is 13 to 18 months old, it goes back to the guide dog center. There it gets more training. Then the puppy is given to a new owner," said Sally.

Have you ever seen a dog like this? It is a guide dog. A guide dog helps people who cannot see. Guide dogs help them walk on busy streets. Guide dogs even know to stop at the top of stairs.

Every effort has been made to secure permission and provide appropriate credit for photographic material. The publisher deeply regrets any omission and pledges to correct errors called to its attention in subsequent editions.

Unless otherwise acknowledged, all photographs are the property of Scott Foresman, a division of Pearson Education.

Photo locators denoted as follows: Top (T), Center (C), Bottom (B), Left (L), Right (R), Background (Bkgd)

1 ©Phanie/Photo Researchers, Inc.; 3 ©Jim Craigmyle/Corbis; 4 Guide Dogs For the Blind, Inc.; 7 ©Stephanie Diani/Corbis; 8 ©Van Parys/Corbis; 9 ©Phanie/Photo Researchers, Inc.; 10 ©Dale C. Spartas/Corbis

ISBN: 0-328-13218-7

2 3 4 5 6 7 8 9 10 V010 14 13 12 11 10 09 08 07 06 05

It was cold. Sally's mother put wood on the fire in the fireplace. She said, "Won't you be sad when it's time to give the dog back?"

"Yes," Sally said. "But knowing that my dog will help someone else will make me feel better."

"So," said Sally, "may I be a puppy raiser?"

Sally's mother took a long look at Sally. What would her mother say?

"Sally," said her mother. "I think you would be a great puppy raiser."

A Puppy Raiser

by Rosa Lester

PEARSON
Scott Foresman

Editorial Offices: Glenview, Illinois • Parsippany, New Jersey • New York, New York
Sales Offices: Needham, Massachusetts • Duluth, Georgia • Glenview, Illinois
Coppell, Texas • Ontario, California • Mesa, Arizona

Vocabulary

door

loved

should

wood

Word count: 437

Note: The total word count includes words in the running text and headings only. Numerals and words in chapter titles, captions, labels, diagrams, charts, graphs, sidebars, and extra features are not included.

Think and Share

Read Together

1. Make a chart like the one below. Write four things Sally tells her mother she can do as a puppy raiser.

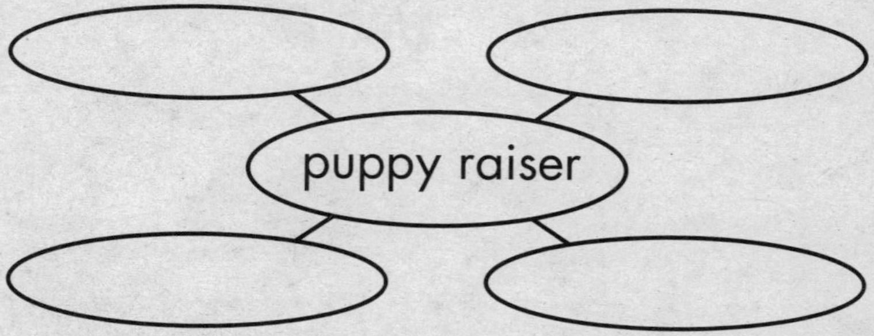

2. Write a few sentences. Tell what a guide dog does.

3. Use each of the vocabulary words in a sentence: *door, loved, should,* and *wood.*

4. Would you like to raise a guide dog? Why or why not?

Suggested levels for Guided Reading, DRA™, Lexile,® and Reading Recovery™ are provided in the Pearson Scott Foresman Leveling Guide.

Social Studies

Genre	Comprehension Skills and Strategy
Narrative nonfiction	• Sequence • Main Idea • Summarize

Scott Foresman Reading Street 1.5.2

ISBN 0-328-13218-7

9 780328 132187 90000

PEARSON
Scott Foresman

scottforesman.com

Social Studies

A Puppy Raiser

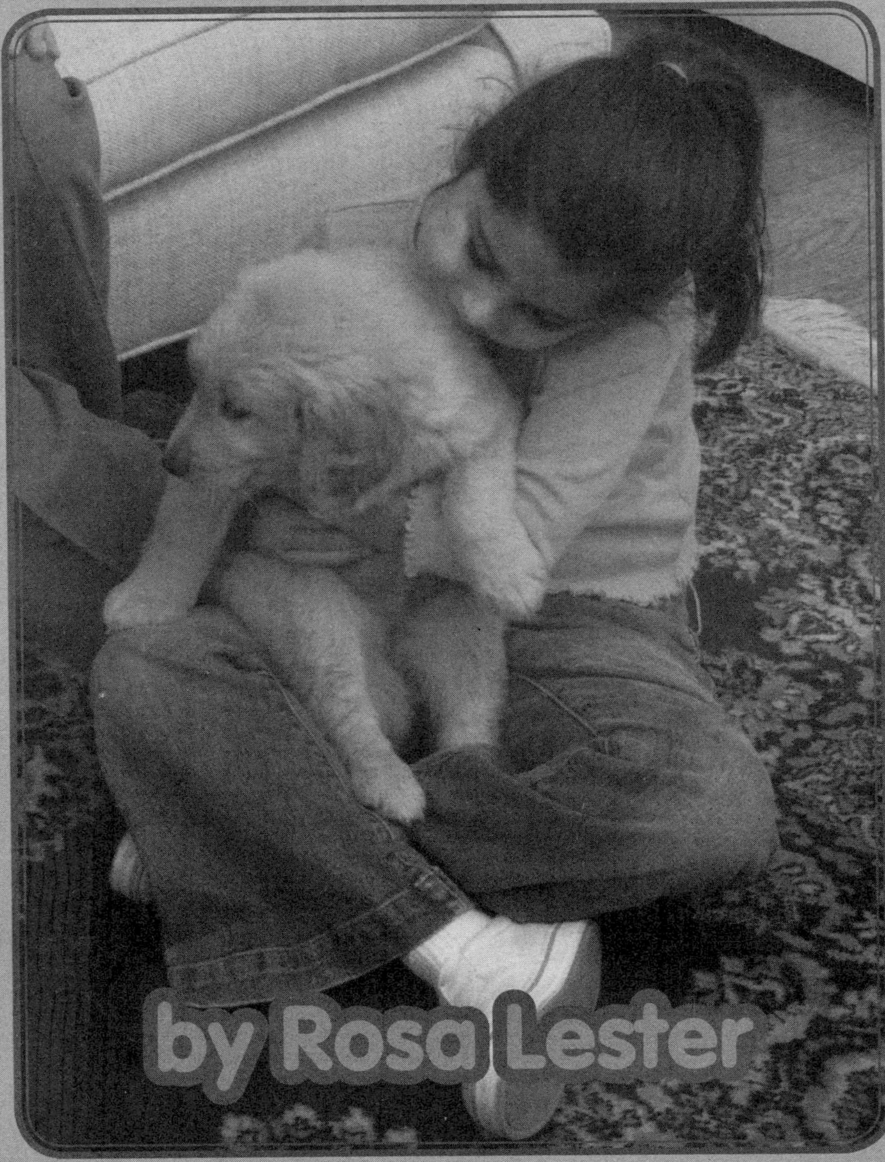

by Rosa Lester

Squirrel tried lifting the pumpkin. It didn't move.

Then he tried pushing the pumpkin. It still didn't move.

Squirrel even tried pulling the pumpkin. Nothing worked. Squirrel could not move that pumpkin.

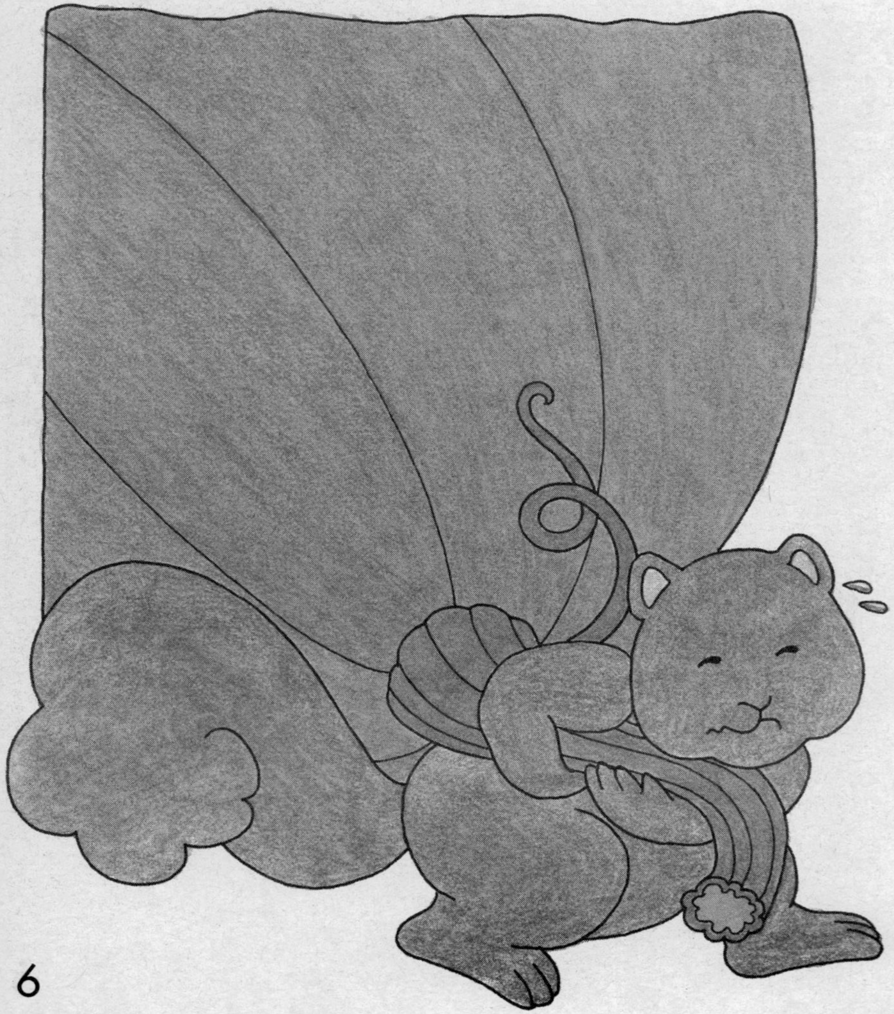

Squirrel was tired. He needed a rest. He lay down and closed his eyes.

Suddenly, he heard a loud noise. It sounded like this: "SNUFFLE!"

Squirrel opened his eyes. Was it the farmer?

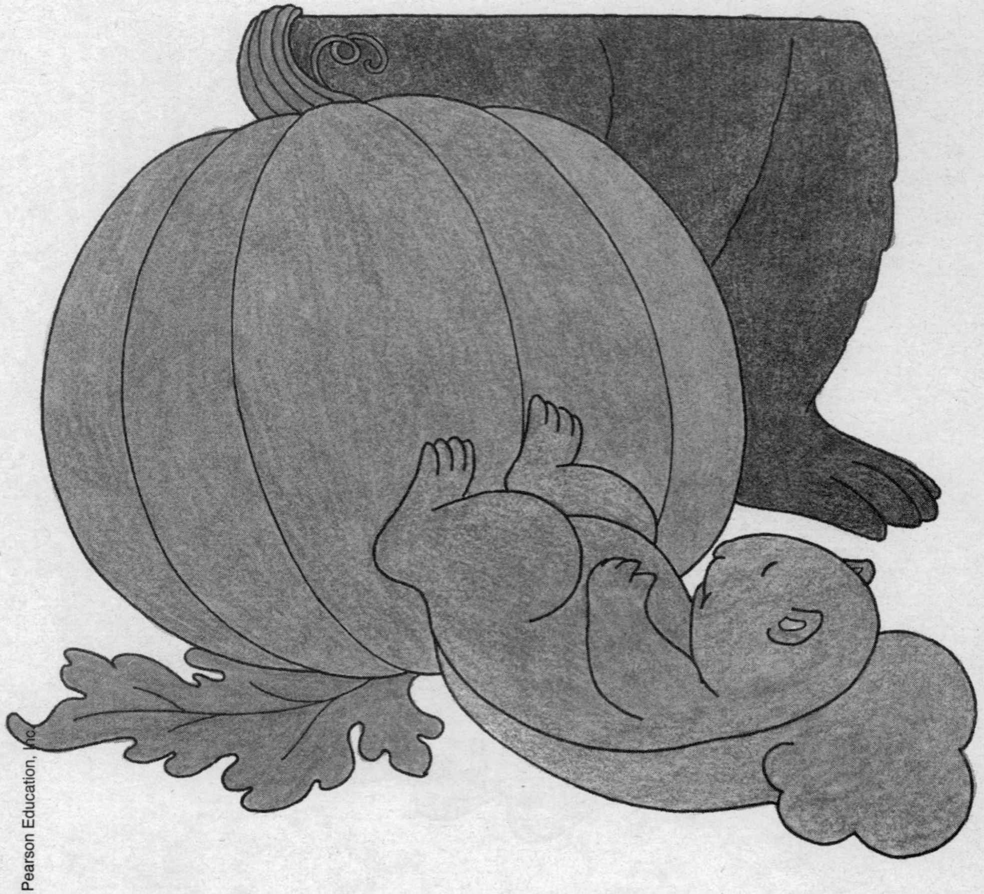

Squirrel peeked around the pumpkin. It was not the farmer. It was a big brown bear.

"Greetings, Bear," said Squirrel. "You look very strong. Will you help me with this pumpkin?"

Squirrel went to the farmer's garden. He sneaked behind a big pumpkin. He looked around. He did not see anyone. It was safe to take the pumpkin.

Squirrel did not have a pumpkin, but he knew where to find one.

Squirrel lived near a farmer who had a pumpkin patch. Farmers never like squirrels in their pumpkin patches. Squirrel would have to make sure the farmer did not see him.

"I do not like pumpkins," said Bear.

"Oh? What do you like?" said Squirrel in a worried voice. "Squirrels?"

"Squirrels are not bad, but apples are my favorite," said Bear.

"Well," Squirrel said. "If you help me, I will give you lots of apples."

Lots of apples sounded good to Bear. So Bear pushed the pumpkin along. She pushed it toward the grass. She pushed it toward the trees. She pushed it all the way to Squirrel's apple tree!

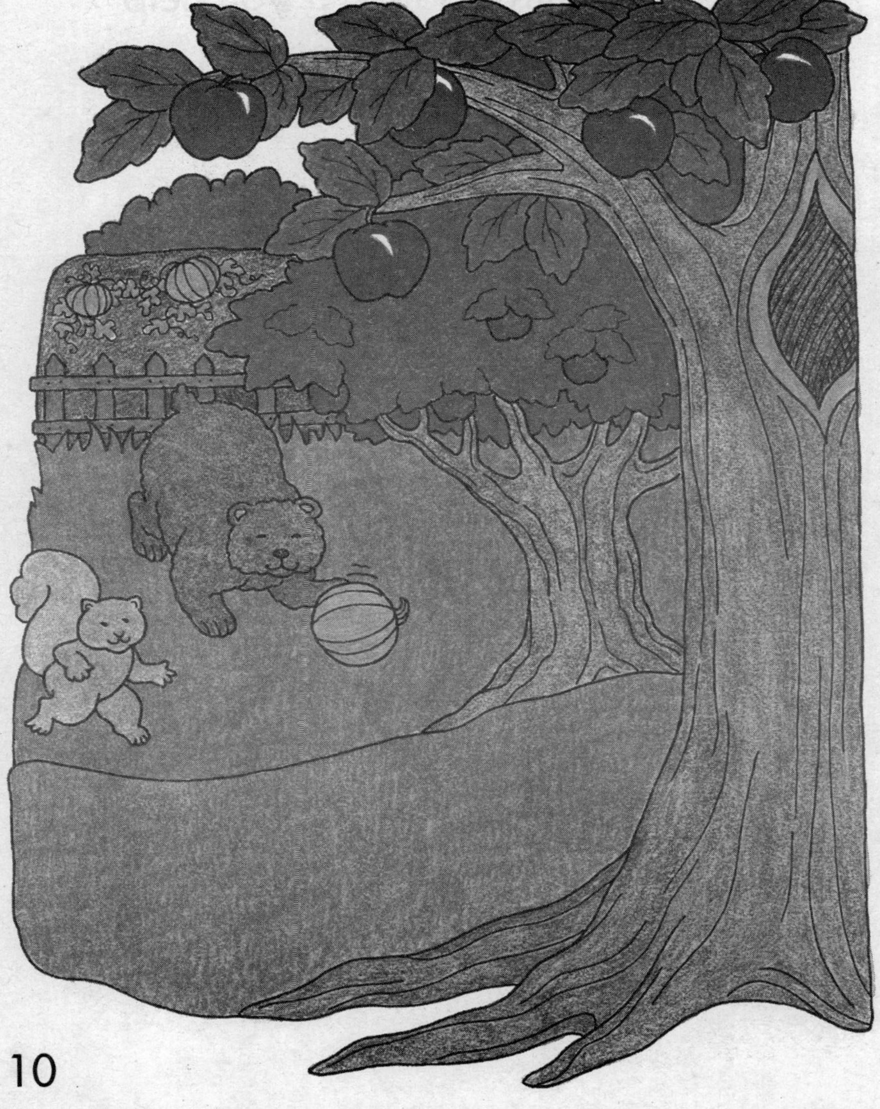

Squirrel sat in his tree. He looked at all his apples. He scowled.

"I am sick of apples," said Squirrel. "I am sick of nuts. I want something new. I want to eat a pumpkin!"

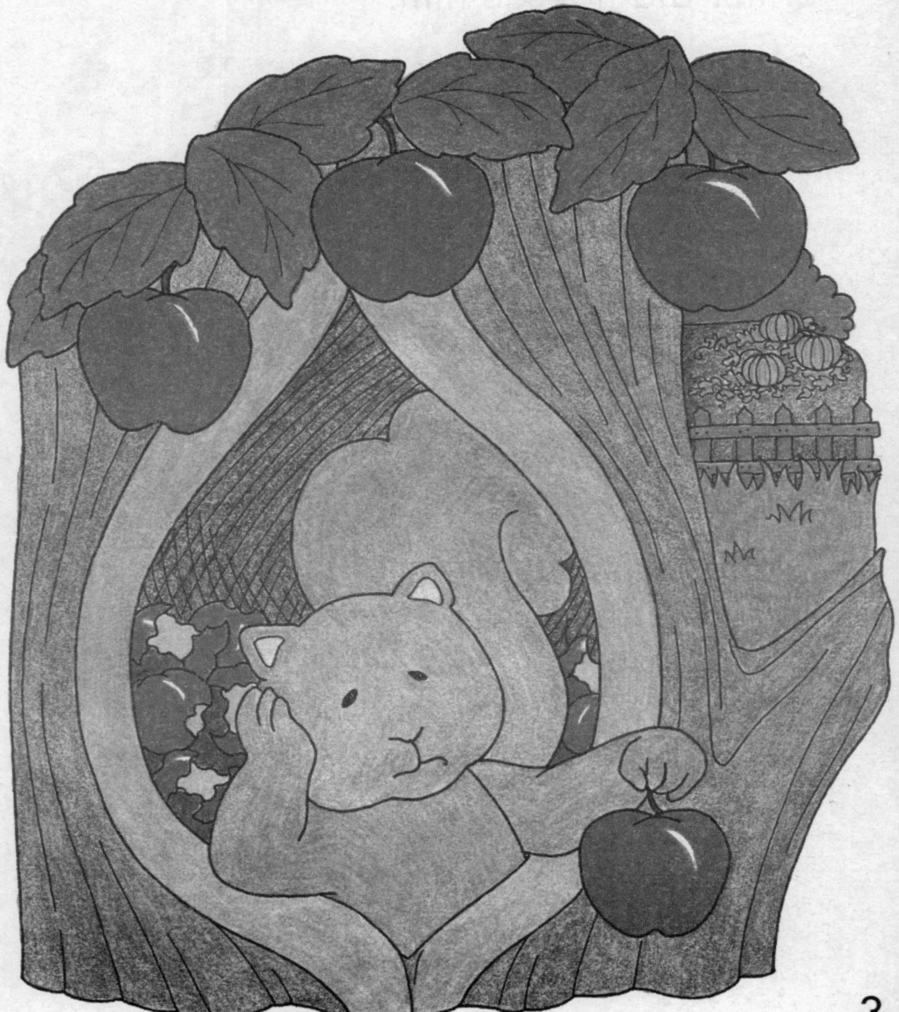

Every effort has been made to secure permission and provide appropriate credit for photographic material. The publisher deeply regrets any omission and pledges to correct errors called to its attention in subsequent editions.

Unless otherwise acknowledged, all photographs are the property of Scott Foresman, a division of Pearson Education.

ISBN: 0-328-13215-2

2 3 4 5 6 7 8 9 10 V010 14 13 12 11 10 09 08 07 06 05

Bear hid the pumpkin behind the tree for Squirrel. Then Squirrel dug in!

"Yum, yum," said Squirrel.

Bear started eating.

"Yum, yum," said Bear.

What a day for Squirrel and Bear!

What Do They Eat?

Read Together

Did you know that some squirrels like pumpkins? Did you know that some bears like fruit?

Squirrels like to eat nuts, seeds, grains, vegetables, and fruit. Pumpkins are tasty, and they are full of yummy seeds! If a squirrel is hungry, it will eat almost any kind of food.

Bears eat both meat and plants. Bears sometimes hunt young deer, elk, or moose. Bears also like to eat berries and grass. Sometimes bears even climb trees to get fruit. Bears eat honey too!

And yes, most bears eat squirrels! In real life, Bear and Squirrel would not be friends.

Pumpkins and Apples

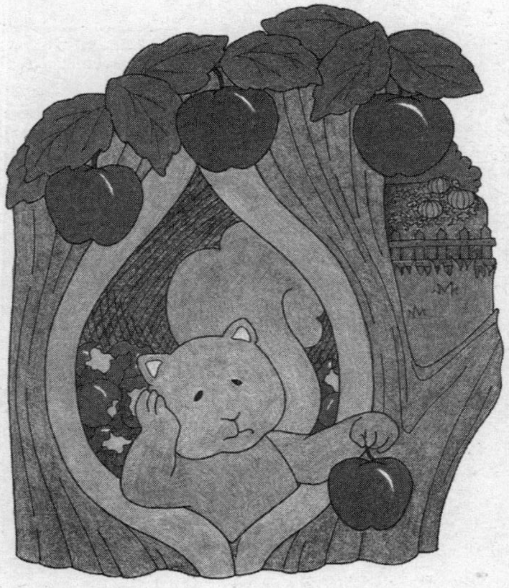

by Gregory Grissom
illustrated by Ginna Magee

PEARSON
Scott Foresman

Editorial Offices: Glenview, Illinois • Parsippany, New Jersey • New York, New York
Sales Offices: Needham, Massachusetts • Duluth, Georgia • Glenview, Illinois
Coppell, Texas • Ontario, California • Mesa, Arizona

Vocabulary

along
behind
eyes
never
pulling
toward

Word count: 311

Note: The total word count includes words in the running text and headings only. Numerals and words in chapter titles, captions, labels, diagrams, charts, graphs, sidebars, and extra features are not included.

Think and Share

Read Together

1. Who are the characters in this story? Where does the story take place?
2. Think about what happened in this story. Use a chart like the one below to tell the plot of this story in the order it happened.

Beginning
↓
Middle
↓
End

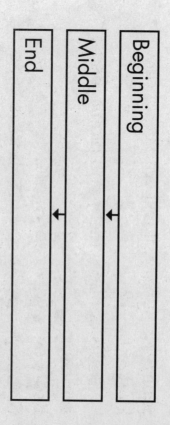

3. Find the word *scowled* on page 3. Draw a picture of a face to show what *scowled* means.
4. Squirrel likes pumpkins best. Bear likes apples. What vegetables and fruits do you like best?

Suggested levels for Guided Reading, DRA™, Lexile,® and Reading Recovery™ are provided in the Pearson Scott Foresman Leveling Guide.

Genre	Comprehension Skills and Strategy
Animal fantasy	• Character, Setting, Plot • Realism and Fantasy • Story Structure

Scott Foresman Reading Street 1.5.1

PEARSON Scott Foresman
scottforesman.com

ISBN 0-328-13215-2
9 780328 132157 90000

Pumpkins and Apples

by Gregory Grissom
illustrated by Ginna Magee

An adult named Debbie Spaide helped with the club. Kids in other towns were told about this club. They thought it was a good idea. They wanted their own Kids Care Clubs.

Soon, other kids across the country opened Kids Care Clubs!

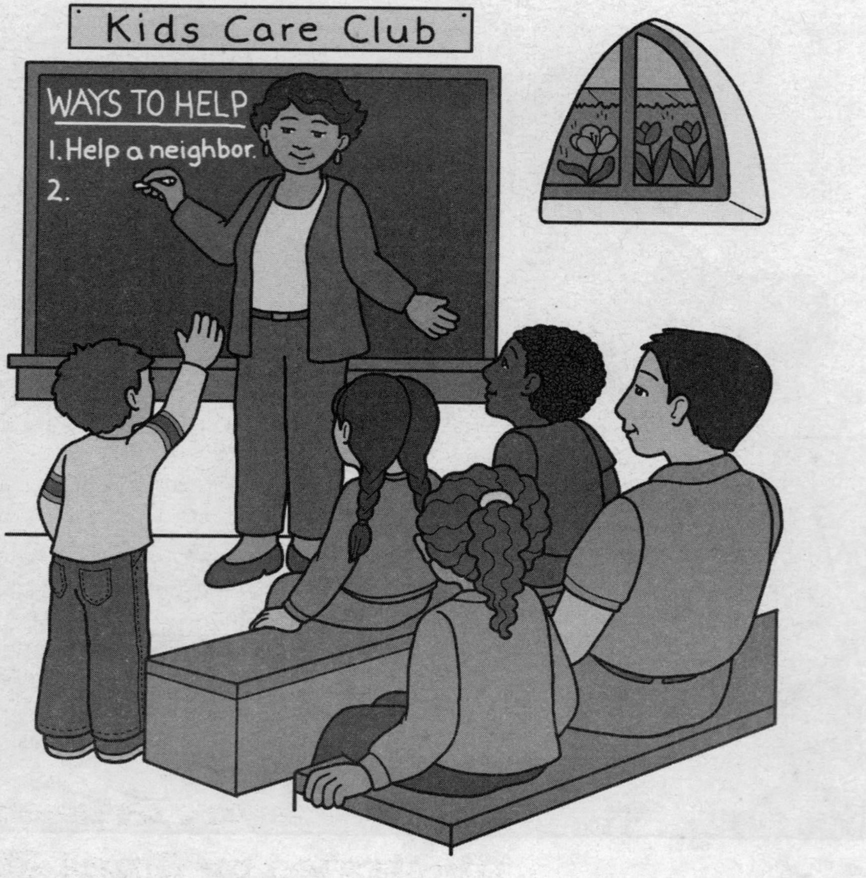

Children join the Kids Care Clubs because they want to help others. Also, it is fun for the kids to get together.

Parents, teachers, and other adults work with the children in Kids Care Clubs. They help the kids find where their help will do the most good.

There is a lot that the kids can do to help. They visit with those who might be lonely. They talk to people and play games. Sometimes, they listen to music and dance.

A few weeks later, the same friends made 150 lunches for people who were not getting enough to eat. This made the people happy. They did not expect it.

The friends liked being helpful. They wanted to do more. They started a club to help others called Kids Care Club.

In 1990, a bunch of friends got together. They wanted to make their neighborhood a better place. They decided to rake the lawn for a neighbor. She was an older woman. She could not rake the leaves herself. She was surprised and happy.

The kids learn a lot from the older people as well. They tell stories to the children about things that happened long ago.

The Kids Care Club visits make both the kids and the older people very happy.

Kids in the Kids Care Clubs also like to help other kids.

They make cards and presents for children who are sick. This cheers the children up and makes them feel better.

What kind of presents would you make for someone who was sick?

Kids can do a lot more than most people think. They can make the world a better place. Here is a true story about kids who are doing just that.

ISBN: 0-328-13212-8

2 3 4 5 6 7 8 9 10 V010 14 13 12 11 10 09 08 07 06 05

Kids Care Clubs don't help only sick children. They help other children who need help, as well.

The Kids Care Clubs collect clothes and shoes. They send these things to children who need them.

Also, kids in the Kids Care Clubs help clean up empty lots near their homes. They collect food for those who need it.

What do you think about Kids Care Clubs? Is it something you would like to do? Maybe your parents or teachers can help you start a Kids Care Club.

The Kids Care Club

by Rosa Lester
illustrated by Ginna Magge

PEARSON
Scott Foresman

Editorial Offices: Glenview, Illinois • Parsippany, New Jersey • New York, New York
Sales Offices: Needham, Massachusetts • Duluth, Georgia • Glenview, Illinois
Coppell, Texas • Ontario, California • Mesa, Arizona

Vocabulary

across
because
dance
only
opened
shoes
told

Word count: 414

Note: The total word count includes words in the running text and headings only. Numerals and words in chapter titles, captions, labels, diagrams, charts, graphs, sidebars, and extra features are not included.

Think and Share

Read Together

1. Why was the first Kids Care Club formed? What happened after that?
2. When you read on page 6 that an adult helped the kids, what did you predict would happen next to the Kids Care Club?
3. Identify the words in this book that end with *–ly* and *–ful* and use each one in a sentence.
4. In what ways are the kids in the Kids Care Club being good citizens? Use examples of the things they do to help.

Suggested levels for Guided Reading, DRA, Lexile,® and Reading Recovery™ are provided in the Pearson Scott Foresman Leveling Guide.

Social Studies

Genre	Comprehension Skills and Strategy
Expository nonfiction	• Cause and Effect • Author's Purpose • Preview the Text

Scott Foresman Reading Street 1.4.6

PEARSON
Scott Foresman
scottforesman.com

ISBN 0-328-13212-8
9 780328 132126 90000

Social Studies

The Kids Care Club

by Rosa Lester
illustrated by Ginna Magge

Drew also likes to eat. He gets pretty messy.

I washed his face. He didn't like that at all. He threw his food.

"Mom," I yelled. "I need help!"

"I remember when you made a mess like that," she said to me. "Let Drew watch you wash your face."

I washed my face. Drew washed his face!

"See," said Mom. "You know what to do with Drew now."

Drew and I were looking at a picture book. The cat came in. Drew grabbed the cat. Drew likes the cat, but I'm not sure that the cat likes Drew.

"Dad," I yelled. "Come here! I need help!"

"I remember when you did that," she said to me. "I bet you can show Drew how to pull up on the sofa."

I took Drew to the sofa. He stood up.

Drew can stand, but he needs help. The other day, I saw him tugging on the drapes to stand. I thought that would be OK, but then, RIP!

"Mom," I yelled. "Come quick! I need help!"

"I remember when you grabbed the cat like that," Dad said. "Can you show Drew the way to pet a cat?"

I took Drew's little hand and helped him pet the cat gently.

"See," Dad said. "You know what to do with Drew now."

Drew has had a busy day. He stood up. He made a mess. He grabbed the cat. Now he needs to sleep, but he isn't sleeping.

I have had a busy day too. I can't sleep. I can hear Drew crying in my room. I know what I can do, and I don't have to call for help this time.

Hi! I'm Sue. This is Drew. He is my little brother.

When Drew was born, he didn't do much. Now that he is big, he does a lot!

Every effort has been made to secure permission and provide appropriate credit for photographic material. The publisher deeply regrets any omission and pledges to correct errors called to its attention in subsequent editions.

Unless otherwise acknowledged, all photographs are the property of Scott Foresman, a division of Pearson Education.

ISBN: 0-328-13209-8

2 3 4 5 6 7 8 9 10 V010 14 13 12 11 10 09 08 07 06 05

I'll sing some quiet songs for Drew, just like Mom and Dad did for me when I was little. He likes that, just like I did.

See! I think he's going to sleep. Good night.

As Babies Grow

Read Together

Babies can be lots of fun. They can be lots of work, too, because they aren't able to do much for themselves. Parents, other family members, or babysitters must hold, feed, bathe, dress, and keep them safe and happy.

After babies grow a bit, and begin to walk, they are no longer babies but are toddlers. Toddlers learn to talk and to do many other things, but they still can't do many of the things you can do. As they grow, toddlers learn to do more and more by watching other people, like you, do things.

Sue and Drew

by Sammie Witt

illustrated by Mike Dammer

PEARSON Scott Foresman

Editorial Offices: Glenview, Illinois • Parsippany, New Jersey • New York, New York
Sales Offices: Needham, Massachusetts • Duluth, Georgia • Glenview, Illinois
Coppell, Texas • Ontario, California • Mesa, Arizona

Vocabulary

picture

remember

room

stood

thought

Word count: 440

Note: The total word count includes words in the running text and headings only. Numerals and words in chapter titles, captions, labels, diagrams, charts, graphs, sidebars, and extra features are not included.

Think and Share

Read Together

1. How does Sue feel about her brother? Why do you think that?

2. Fold a sheet of paper into three parts like the picture shows. Then draw or write about the beginning, the middle, and the end parts of the story you just read.

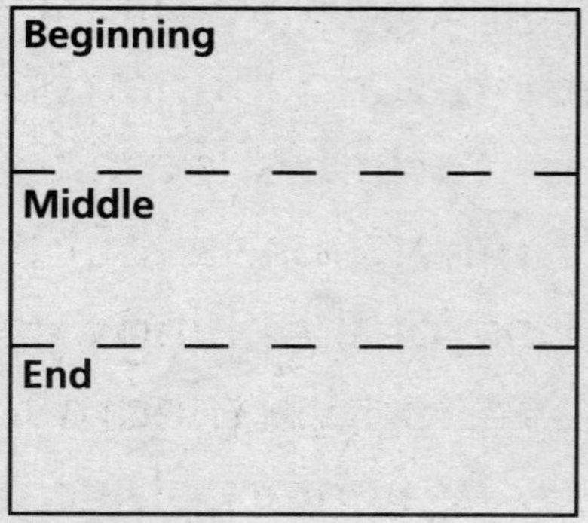

3. On a separate paper, draw or write your answers to these three questions:

- Where did the story happen?
- Who were the two characters the story was mostly about, and how are they related?
- What happened to them in the story?

4. What would you do to help a toddler learn how to behave?

Suggested levels for Guided Reading, DRA,™ Lexile,® and Reading Recovery™ are provided in the Pearson Scott Foresman Leveling Guide.

Genre	Comprehension Skills and Strategy
Realistic fiction	• Character, Setting, Plot • Realism and Fantasy • Story Structure

Scott Foresman Reading Street 1.4.5

PEARSON
Scott Foresman
scottforesman.com

ISBN 0-328-13209-8
9 780328 132096 90000

Sue and Drew

by Sammie Witt

illustrations by Mike Dammer

"Thanksgiving is a time to be with your family and friends. We say thanks for everything we have. We eat a big feast with turkey, potatoes, and pies," Jane said.

"I love pie," said Ling.

"My mom makes three kinds of pies," said Jane. "I write the name of each pie on a card."

"That sounds yummy," said Ling. "We don't have Thanksgiving in China. But we do have a holiday like it."

"It is the Moon Festival," said Ling.

"It is a big holiday for the Chinese people. It comes at harvest time."

"That is like Thanksgiving!" said Jane.

"The festival is on the night with the brightest full moon," said Ling. "It looks so big, you feel like you can touch it!"

Jane said, "The first Thanksgiving was at harvest time. That was when the crops were picked. People were happy that they had food to eat. They made a big feast and shared it with friends."

Ling was happy to be with Jane's family. She was excited about Thanksgiving.

"I don't know about Thanksgiving," said Ling as she unpacked her things. "We don't have that holiday in China."

"What happens then?" asked Jane.

"Families get together," said Ling. "We watch the full moon high above us. We talk and sing moon songs in the bright light. But we don't eat turkey or pie. We eat moon cakes!"

"Moon cakes are made from bean paste. Some cakes have a cooked egg yolk inside. It looks like a bright, yellow moon," Ling said.

"Do they taste good?" asked Jane

Ling gave a happy laugh. "Oh, yes. One time, I had eight and then my tummy hurt."

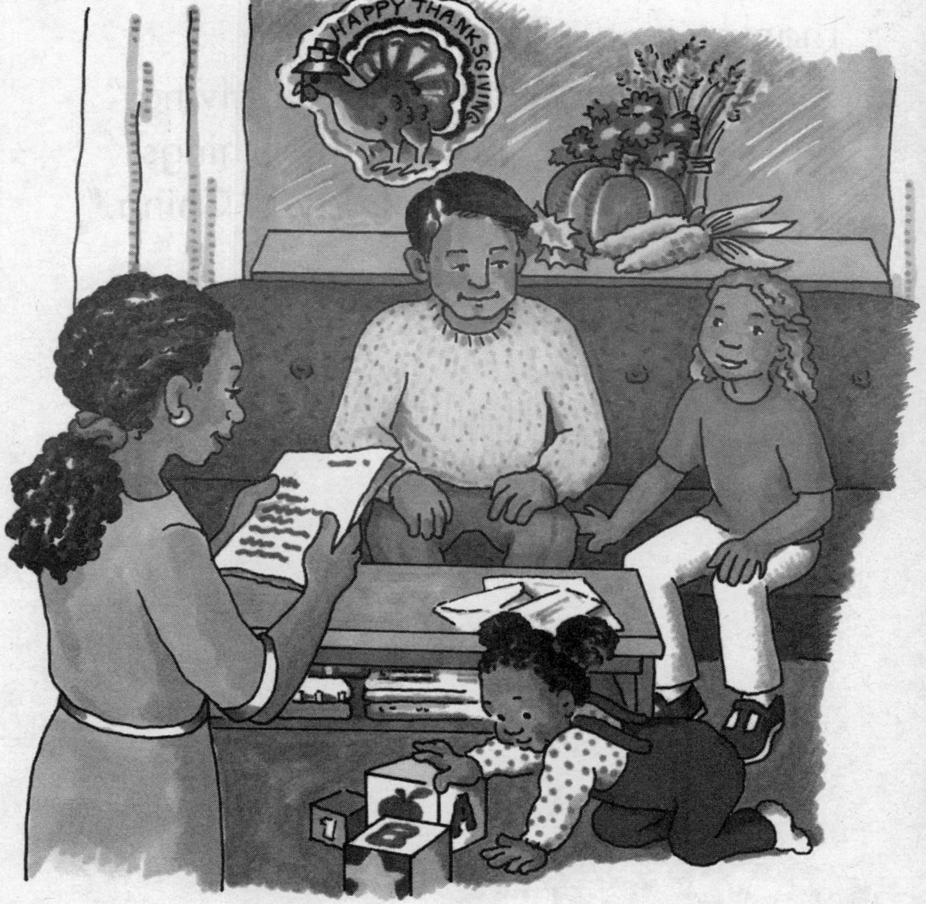

It was almost Thanksgiving. Thanksgiving was eight-year-old Jane's favorite holiday.

"My friend Ling will visit," said Jane's mother. "She lives far away in China."

Every effort has been made to secure permission and provide appropriate credit for photographic material. The publisher deeply regrets any omission and pledges to correct errors called to its attention in subsequent editions.

Unless otherwise acknowledged, all photographs are the property of Scott Foresman, a division of Pearson Education.

Photo locators denoted as follows: Top (T), Center (C), Bottom (B), Left (L), Right (R), Background (Bkgd)

12 (B) CHINA PHOTOS/Reuters/Corbis

ISBN: 0-328-13206-3

2 3 4 5 6 7 8 9 10 V010 14 13 12 11 10 09 08 07 06 05

"The Moon Festival sounds like fun," said Jane.

"It is," said Ling. "It is a real treasure. Maybe one day you will visit me when it is festival time."

"That would be great!" said Jane.

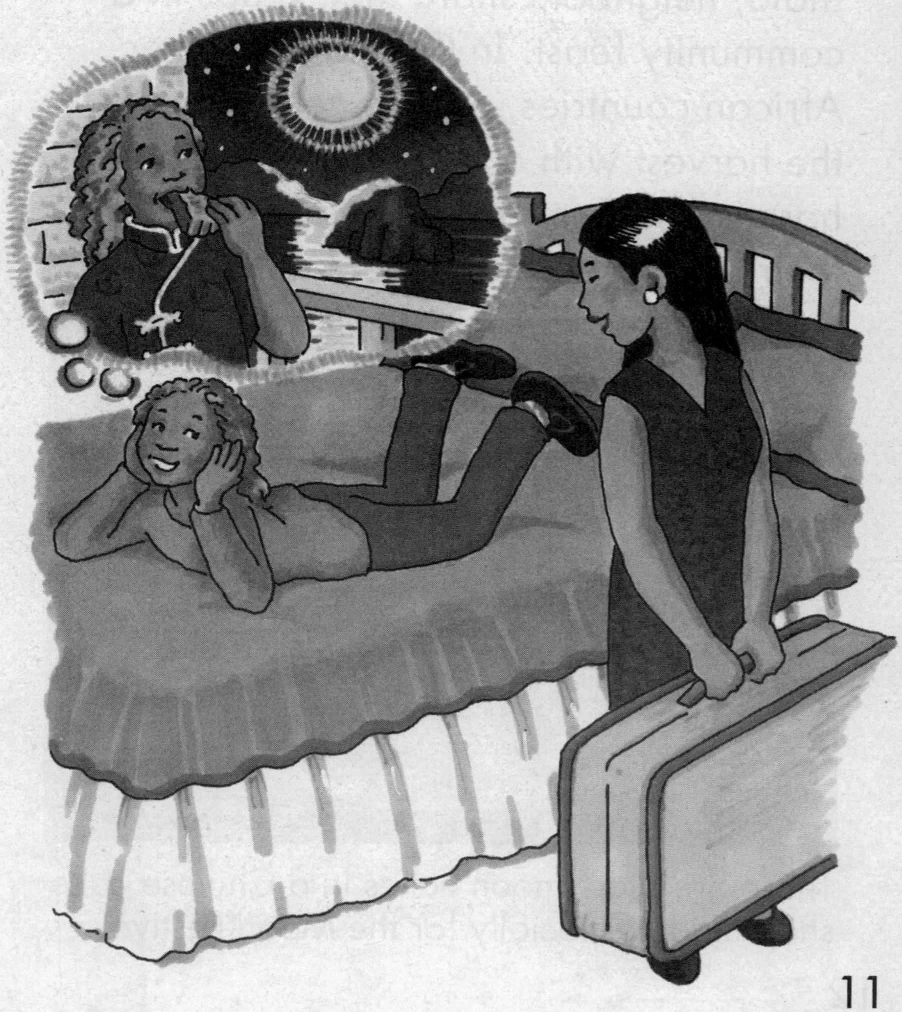

Harvest Holidays

Read Together

Harvest time is celebrated in many cultures. In Vietnam, there is also a moon festival. Like the Chinese, people eat moon cakes under the moon. In India, neighbors share their crops in a community feast. In Ghana and other African countries, people celebrate the harvest with a yam festival. People harvest the yams and then share with their friends and family.

These are giant moon cakes in a Chinese cake shop made especially for the Moon Festival.

Harvest Holidays

by Rowan Obach
illustrated by Corasue Nicholas

PEARSON Scott Foresman

Editorial Offices: Glenview, Illinois • Parsippany, New Jersey • New York, New York
Sales Offices: Needham, Massachusetts • Duluth, Georgia • Glenview, Illinois
Coppell, Texas • Ontario, California • Mesa, Arizona

Vocabulary

above
eight
laugh
moon
touch

Word count: 399

Note: The total word count includes words in the running text and headings only. Numerals and words in chapter titles, captions, labels, diagrams, charts, graphs, sidebars, and extra features are not included.

Think and Share

Read Together

1. Could this story really happen? Why do you think so?

2. On page 9 of the story, Ling says, "We eat moon cakes!" If you weren't sure what moon cakes were, what could you do?

3. Which of these words means about the same as feast?

trip meal song

Make a web like the one below to describe a Thanksgiving feast.

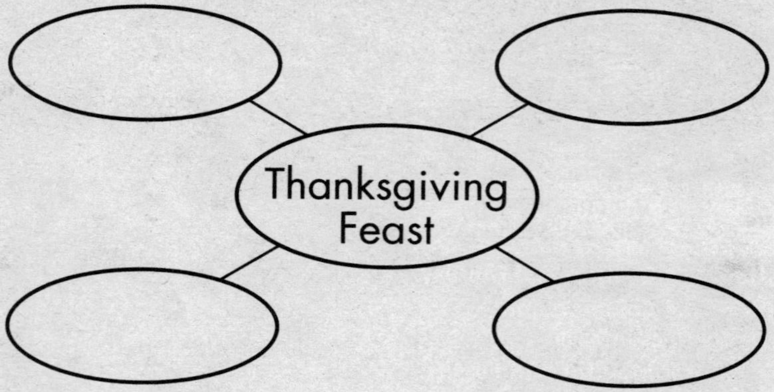

4. What other holidays do you like? Compare those holidays with the Chinese Moon Festival and Thanksgiving. How are they the same? How are they different?

Suggested levels for Guided Reading, DRA,™ Lexile,® and Reading Recovery™ are provided in the Pearson Scott Foresman Leveling Guide.

Genre	Comprehension Skills and Strategy
Realistic fiction	• Realism and Fantasy • Compare and Contrast • Monitor and Fix-Up

Scott Foresman Reading Street 1.4.4

PEARSON
Scott Foresman
scottforesman.com

ISBN 0-328-13206-3
9 780328 132065 90000

Harvest Holidays

by Rowan Obach
illustrated by Corasue Nicholas

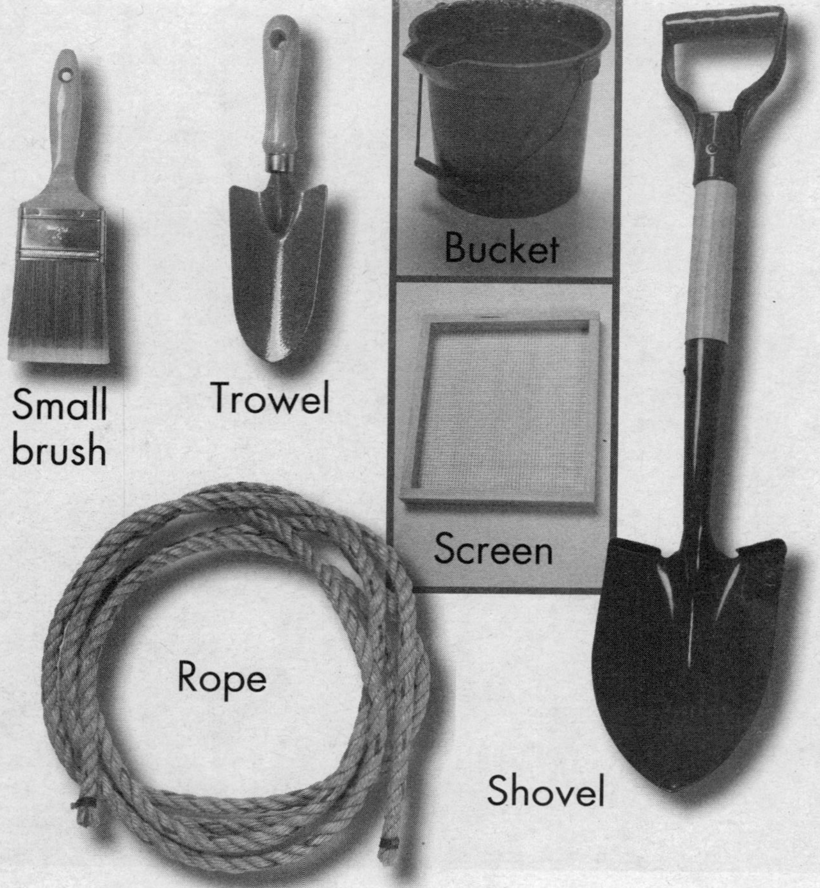

The team must dig through many layers of soil. They might use a shovel, but not for long. Fossils can fall apart. To dig carefully, they use a trowel. Their goal is to save the fossil.

If you want to look for fossils, try this:

1. Put a screen over a bucket. Scoop soil from your dig onto the screen.

2. If you have found a fossil, it will stay on the screen. What do you think you may have found?

The shape of a fossil helps tell the story of the fossil. A fossil of a dinosaur tooth can tell us what the dinosaur ate.

Paleontologists look for fossils in old, old rocks.

First, the digging team finds a place to dig. Once they have found a good place, they rope it off in the shape of a square. Then they start to dig. What tools do you think they use?

Fossils can be bones of animals from a long time ago. Or a fossil can be a wild animal footprint that has turned to stone.

Scientists called paleontologists dig for fossils and study them.

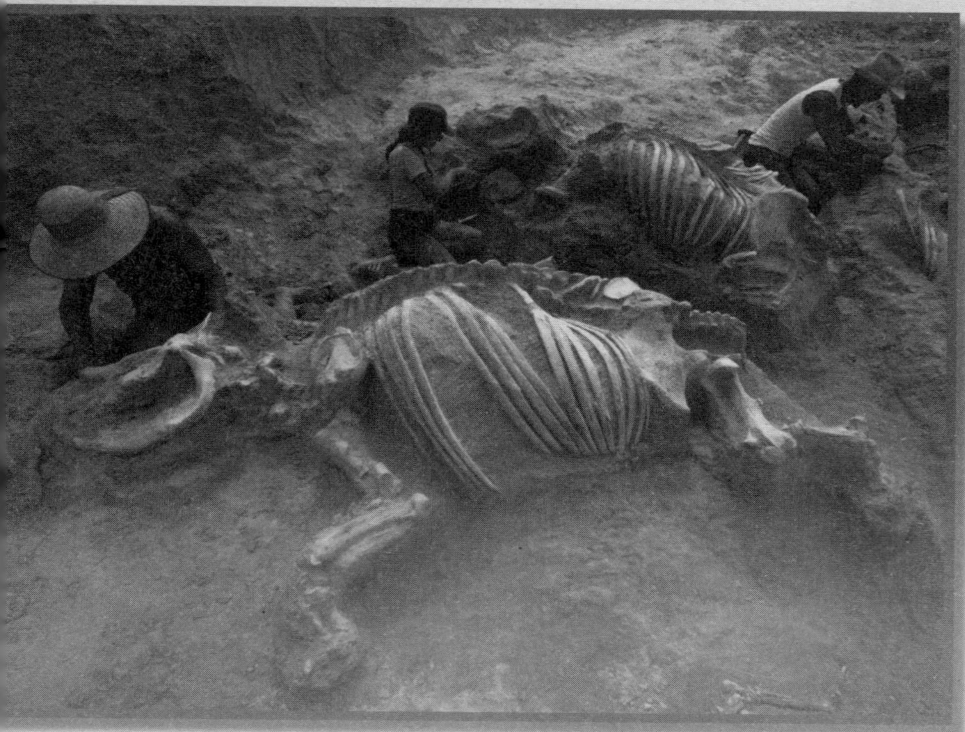

Fossils of dinosaur teeth show us that some dinosaurs ate meat, and some dinosaurs ate plants. Sharp, pointed teeth are from the mouth of a meat-eating dinosaur. Flat, leaf-like teeth are from the mouth of a plant-eating dinosaur.

Flat, leaf-like teeth = plant eaters

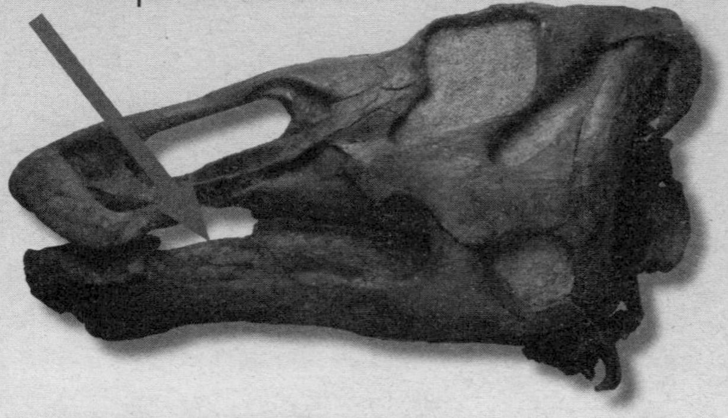

Sharp, pointed teeth = meat eaters

Paleontologists have found fossils of dinosaur eggs in China and Africa. Sometimes these eggs are in a nest. Sometimes they look like big rocks, not eggs!

We are going on a dinosaur dig. We have to bring tools.

What is a dinosaur dig? It is a dig for fossils.

Every effort has been made to secure permission and provide appropriate credit for photographic material. The publisher deeply regrets any omission and pledges to correct errors called to its attention in subsequent editions.

Unless otherwise acknowledged, all photographs are the property of Scott Foresman, a division of Pearson Education.

Photo locators denoted as follows: Top (T), Center (C), Bottom (B), Left (L), Right (R), Background (Bkgd)

CVR ©Annie Griffiths Belt/Corbis; 1 ©Kevin Schafer/Corbis; 3 ©Richard T. Nowitz/Corbis; 4 ©Annie Griffiths Belt/Corbis; 5 ©Richard T. Nowitz/Corbis; 8 (T) ©Kevin Schafer/Corbis: (B) ©Royalty-Free/Corbis; 9 (T) ©DK Limited/Corbis: 9 (B) ©Louie Psihoyos/Corbis; 10 ©Louie Psihoyos/Corbis; 11 ©Duthiel Didier/Corbis; 12 Field Museum of Natural History

ISBN: 0-328-13203-9

2 3 4 5 6 7 8 9 10 V010 14 13 12 11 10 09 08 07 06 05

Not every rock or bone in the earth is a fossil. But if you are lucky and find a fossil, you should share it. Many paleontologists share fossils they find. Just look at the next page.

The paleontologist who found this fossil took it to a museum. That's where you can see it.

Fossils can be found in many places. Maybe you can find one in your own backyard!

Going On a Dinosaur Dig

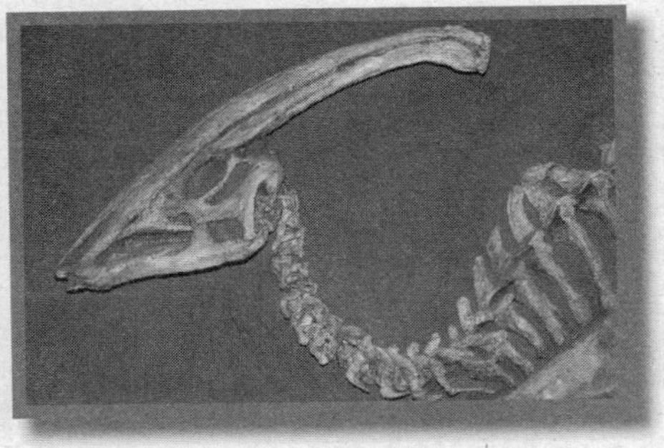

by Kelly Kong

PEARSON
Scott Foresman

Editorial Offices: Glenview, Illinois • Parsippany, New Jersey • New York, New York
Sales Offices: Needham, Massachusetts • Duluth, Georgia • Glenview, Illinois
Coppell, Texas • Ontario, California • Mesa, Arizona

Vocabulary

found
mouth
once
took
wild

Word count: 342

Note: The total word count includes words in the running text and headings only. Numerals and words in chapter titles, captions, labels, diagrams, charts, graphs, sidebars, and extra features are not included.

Think and Share

Read Together

1. What would you like to ask the author about the book she wrote? Use the chart to help you.

K What we know	W What we want to know	L What we learned

2. Where would you look to find out more about dinosaur fossils?
3. *Paleontologist* and *fossil* are big words. Look back in the book to find what they mean. Use each word in a sentence.
4. Look back in your book. Tell how the teeth of meat-eating dinosaurs look.

Suggested levels for Guided Reading, DRA™, Lexile,® and Reading Recovery™ are provided in the Pearson Scott Foresman Leveling Guide.

Science

Genre	Comprehension Skills and Strategy	Text Features
Expository nonfiction	• Author's Purpose • Cause and Effect • Monitor and Fix Up	• Labels

Scott Foresman Reading 1.4.3

ISBN 0-328-13203-9

PEARSON Scott Foresman

scottforesman.com

Science

Earth Science

Going On a Dinosaur Dig

by Kelly Kong

"What does that mean?" her friends asked.

Beth took out her drawing pad. "I need to draw that bird," she said.

So Beth drew. She drew straight lines. She drew curved lines. She drew squiggles. "There!" she said. "Let me show you! Here is a beak, and feet, and wings."

"That's great!" her friends cried. "But look! It is starting to rain. We have to go."

Beth did not seem to hear them.

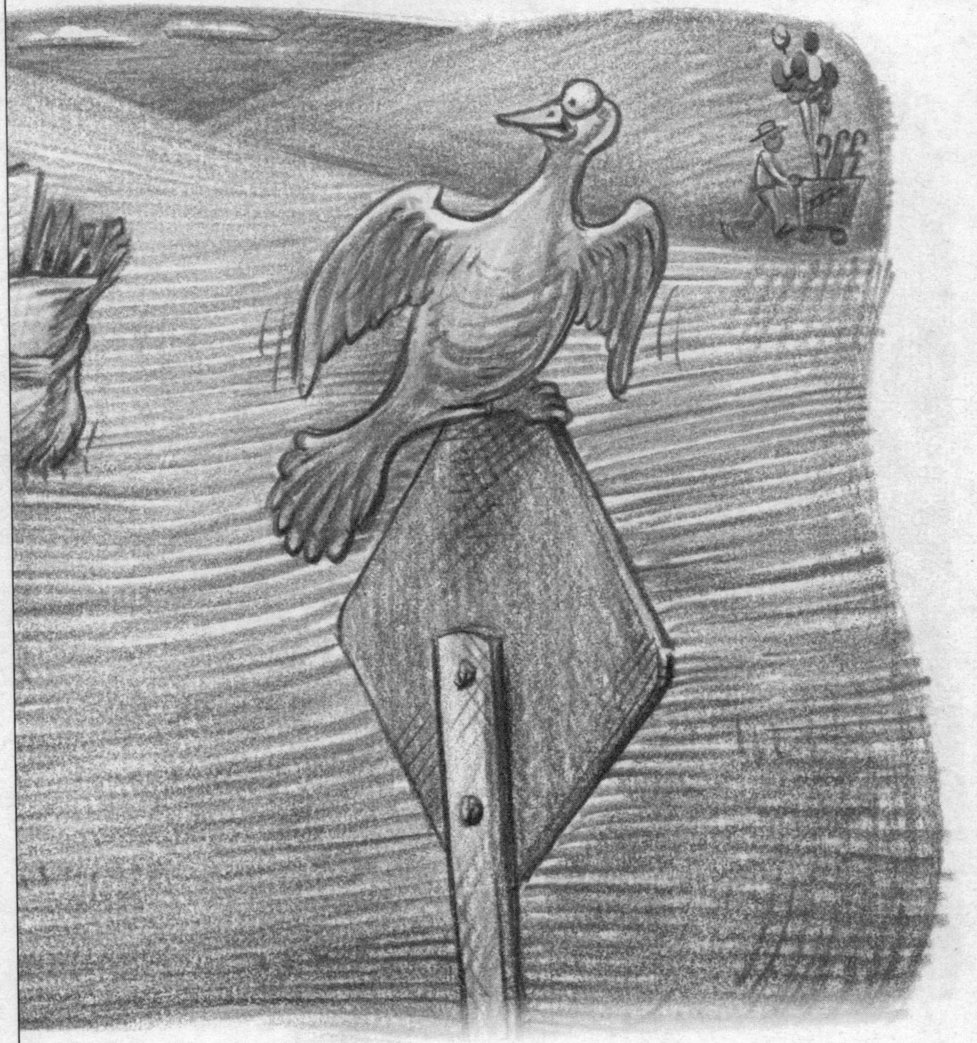

Beth did not speak. She was looking at a bird. It had landed on a sign. Beth just stared.

"I have a feeling," Beth said at last.

Beth's friends talked about sports, and they talked about movies. But Beth was not talking. She was looking away.

"Beth?" they called to her.

"Now for the colors," Beth said. She got out her paints. She painted straight lines. She painted curved lines. She painted squiggles. She stepped back and looked at her painting.

"But it isn't what I feel," Beth said.

Just then, Beth saw a feather. She picked it up. She dipped it in the paint and painted with it.

At last, Beth was done. "Perfect," she said. "Now I'll wait until the paint dries."

Beth and her friends were eating lunch in the park.

"Tell us about your trip to the beach," Beth said to one of her friends.

"It was great!" her friend said.

Every effort has been made to secure permission and provide appropriate credit for photographic material. The publisher deeply regrets any omission and pledges to correct errors called to its attention in subsequent editions.

Unless otherwise acknowledged, all photographs are the property of Scott Foresman, a division of Pearson Education.

ISBN: 0-328-13200-4

2 3 4 5 6 7 8 9 10 V010 14 13 12 11 10 09 08 07 06 05

Beth's friends tried to speak to her again, but she did not hear them. She was looking over there at a squirrel. Beth just stared.

"I have a feeling," she said at last.

"Oh, no! We know what that means!" cried Beth's friends together.

Be an Art Detective

Read Together

Did you know that you can decide what a picture is about? Look closely at the picture. If the picture is a painting or photo, think about what you see. What is happening? What kind of feeling does it give you? Think about the colors. Look for shapes and patterns. Now, say what you think the artwork is about.

Here is an example of abstract art.

How Beth Feels

by Melissa Blackwell Burke
illustrated by Gary Krejca

PEARSON Scott Foresman

Editorial Offices: Glenview, Illinois • Parsippany, New Jersey • New York, New York
Sales Offices: Needham, Massachusetts • Duluth, Georgia • Glenview, Illinois
Coppell, Texas • Ontario, California • Mesa, Arizona

Vocabulary

colors
draw
drew
great
over
show
sign

Word count: 272

Note: The total word count includes words in the running text and headings only. Numerals and words in chapter titles, captions, labels, diagrams, charts, graphs, sidebars, and extra features are not included.

Think and Share

Read Together

1. What is the big idea of this story?
2. Use a story map. Write what happened in the story at the beginning, in the middle, and at the end.

   Title: How Beth Feels

   Beginning
   ↓
   Middle
   ↓
   End

3. *Great* is a vocabulary word in this story. Write it on a piece of paper. Then write a word that means the same thing.
4. How does Beth come up with ideas for her art? Use details from the story to explain your answer.

Suggested levels for Guided Reading, DRA, Lexile,® and Reading Recovery™ are provided in the Pearson Scott Foresman Leveling Guide.

Genre	Comprehension Skills and Strategy
Realistic fiction	• Theme • Plot • Graphic Organizers

Scott Foresman Reading Street 1.4.2

PEARSON
Scott Foresman
scottforesman.com

ISBN 0-328-13200-4
9 780328 132003 90000

How Beth Feels

by Melissa Blackwell Burke

illustrated by Gary Krejca

France

People in France make a special cake called *cake for a king*. This cake has a surprise inside. The cake's surprise is a tiny doll.

Would you be surprised to find a doll in your cake? If you get the piece of cake that has the doll, you get a gold crown. You get to be king or queen for the day.

If you don't get the doll, don't worry. You can still have fun eating the cake.

Mexico

In Mexico, a party is called a *fiesta*. Fiestas are all about fun. There are many different foods at a fiesta. A boy watches the cook stir a big pot of *carnitas*.

Zong zi are a kind of rice ball. They are wrapped in bamboo leaves. The bamboo leaves give the rice balls their special flavor.

Some of the rice balls have fruit inside. Others have meat or beans.

China

In China, people celebrate the Dragon Boat Festival. They sail in boats that look like dragons. On this day, everyone eats *zong zi*.

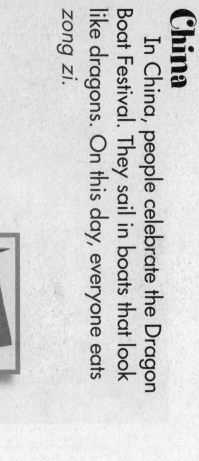

This girl eats a corncob. A band plays, and everyone eats and dances at a fiesta. Which foods would you enjoy eating?

Cuba

Our last stop is Cuba.

A woman is making fresh fruit shakes. They are colorful and sweet. These fruit shakes make any celebration fun.

Cubans also like guava. They make a sweet paste from it to put in desserts.

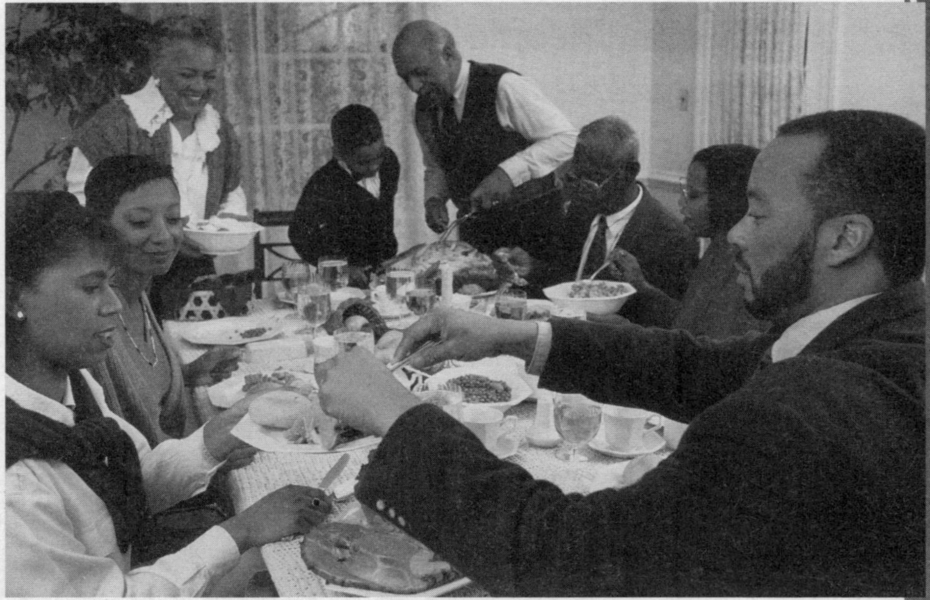

These people are at a Thanksgiving party.

Do you enjoy parties? Do you like eating special foods at your parties?

People all over the world have parties with special foods. Let's take a trip and find out about some of these foods.

Every effort has been made to secure permission and provide appropriate credit for photographic material. The publisher deeply regrets any omission and pledges to correct errors called to its attention in subsequent editions.

Unless otherwise acknowledged, all photographs are the property of Scott Foresman, a division of Pearson Education.

Photo locators denoted as follows: Top (T), Center (C), Bottom (B), Left (L), Right (R), Background (Bkgd)

Cover ©David Turnley/CORBIS; 3 ©Chuck Savage/CORBIS; 4(T) Royalty-Free/CORBIS, (B)©Karen Su/CORBIS; 7(B) ©Dave G. Houser/CORBIS; 8(T) ©David Seawell/CORBIS; 8(B) ©Danny Lehman/CORBIS; 9(T) ©David Turnley/CORBIS, (BL) Hemera Technologies; 10(B) Condé Nast Archive/CORBIS; 11 ©Condé Nast Archive/CORBIS

ISBN: 0-328-13197-0

2 3 4 5 6 7 8 9 10 V010 14 13 12 11 10 09 08 07 06 05

At a birthday party everyone is given a special drink. It is made from orange juice, milk, and sugar. It is very good.

Would you like to try this drink? If so, just turn the page.

A Recipe

Read Together

To make the orange milk drink, you will need:

$\frac{1}{2}$ cup of cold orange juice

$\frac{1}{2}$ cup of cold milk

1 tablespoon of sugar

Put everything in a tall glass.

Stir until it is mixed.

Add some ice.

Enjoy!

Special Days, Special Food

by Juan Lester

PEARSON
Scott Foresman

Editorial Offices: Glenview, Illinois • Parsippany, New Jersey • New York, New York
Sales Offices: Needham, Massachusetts • Duluth, Georgia • Glenview, Illinois
Coppell, Texas • Ontario, California • Mesa, Arizona

Vocabulary

about
enjoy
gives
surprise
surprised
worry
would

Word count: 306

Note: The total word count includes words in the running text and headings only. Numerals and words in chapter titles, captions, labels, diagrams, charts, graphs, sidebars, and extra features are not included.

Think and Share

Read Together

1. Why do people all over the world enjoy special celebrations?
2. If you are reading and don't understand something, what can you do to find out the meaning?
3. Make a chart like the one below. Choose three of these words: *about, gives, surprise, would, enjoy, worry*. Write one word in each box on the left. Use the word in a sentence, or draw a picture in the box on the right, to show what the word means. One is done for you.

Words	Sentence or picture
about	My mom told me about the party.

4. Which celebration would you most like to take part in? Tell why.

Suggested levels for Guided Reading, DRA,™ Lexile,® and Reading Recovery™ are provided in the Pearson Scott Foresman Leveling Guide.

Social Studies

Genre	Comprehension Skills and Strategy	Text Features
Expository nonfiction	• Draw Conclusions • Author's Purpose • Monitor and Fix Up	• Captions • Headings

Scott Foresman Reading Street 1.4.1

PEARSON Scott Foresman

scottforesman.com

ISBN 0-328-13197-0

Social Studies

Special Days, Special Food

by Juan Lester

In the winter, this fox's coat gets white.
It looks just like the snow.

In the summer, its fur gets brown.
It looks just like the ground.

winter

summer

In the winter, how does this bird change?
It grows bumps on the edges of its feet!
Then it won't sink in the deepest snow.

winter

In the winter, the hedge has no roses.

It gets warmer in the spring.
Then roses grow on the hedge.

winter

spring

In the spring, the bear wakes up.
Oh, good-bye, den!
That's right. It's time to eat again.

In the fall, a bear eats and eats.
The bear needs fat before it snows.
The bear sleeps all winter in its
warm den.

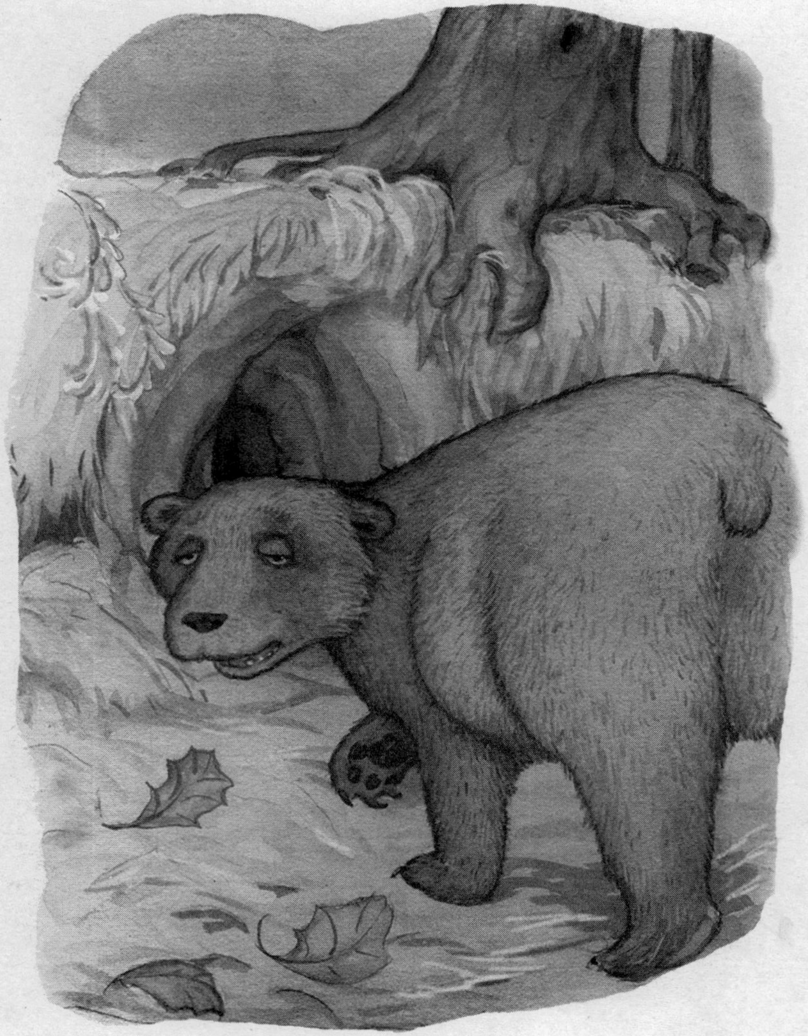

In the spring, an apple tree grows
white flowers.

In the summer and fall, its apples grow.
They can be red, green, or yellow.

spring

fall

Trees need the summer sun.
It helps their leaves get green.

In the fall, the days get shorter.
The leaves turn colors and fall off.

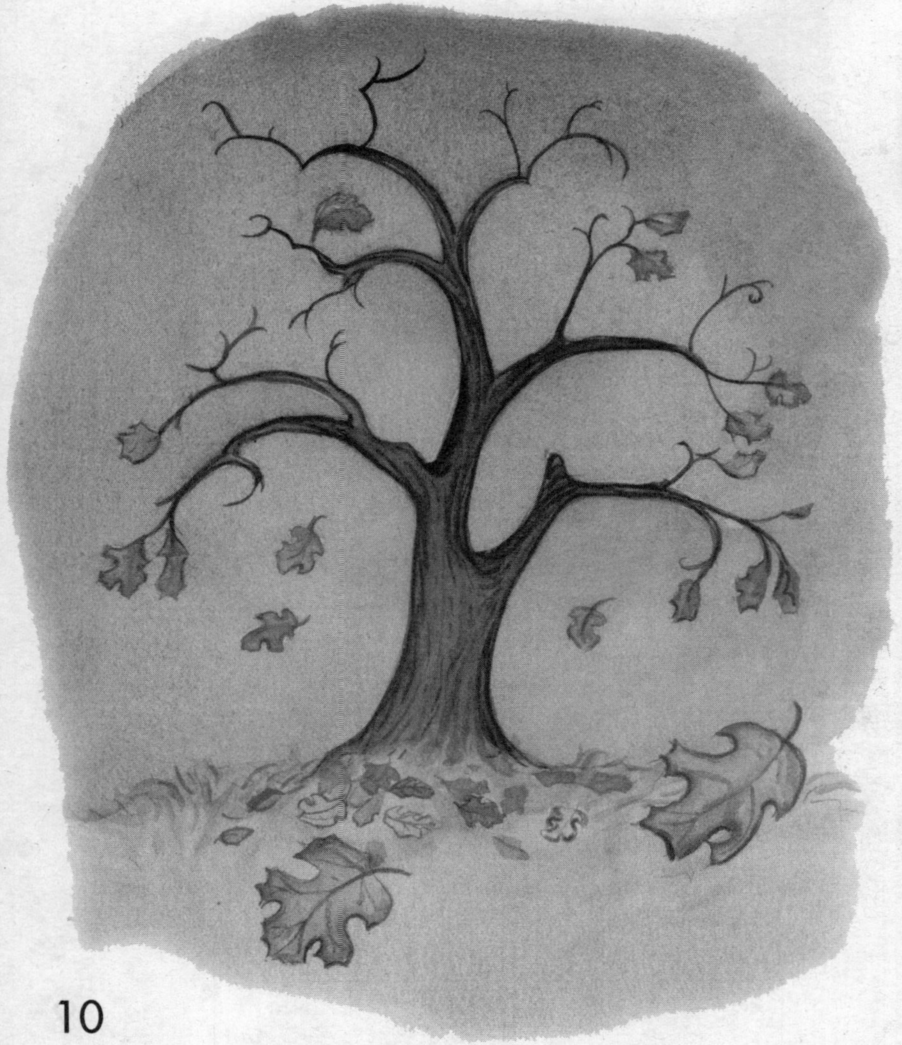

Seasons come and go.
People change their ways.

Animals and plants change too.
Let's find out how.

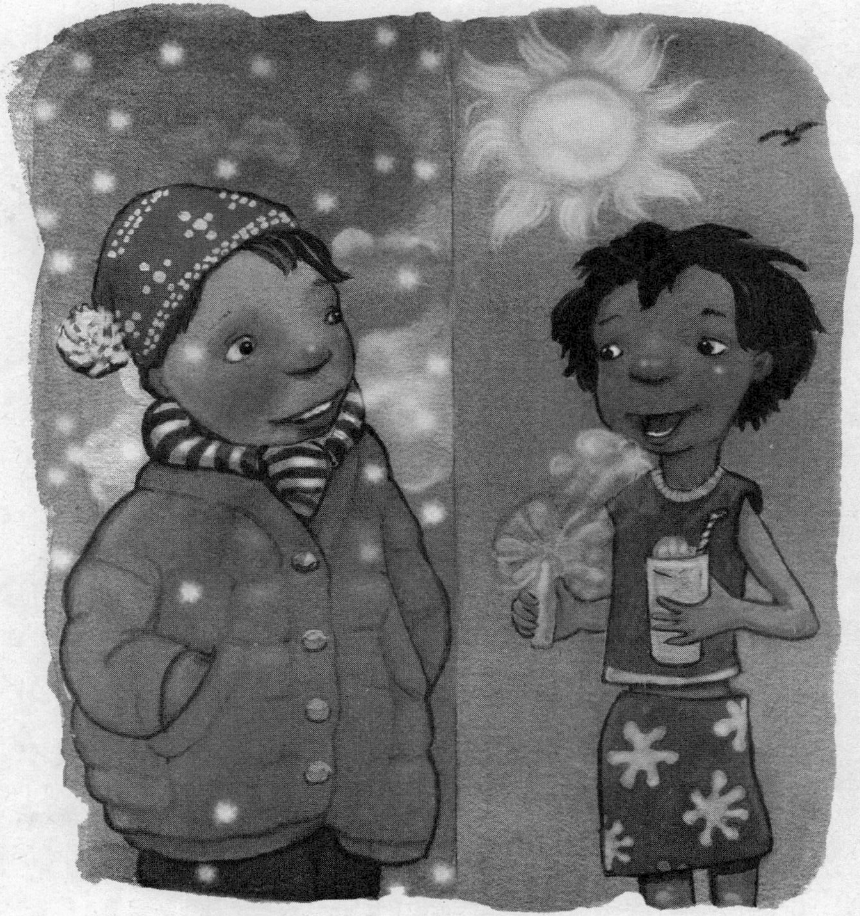

Every effort has been made to secure permission and provide appropriate credit for photographic material. The publisher deeply regrets any omission and pledges to correct errors called to its attention in subsequent editions.

Unless otherwise acknowledged, all photographs are the property of Scott Foresman, a division of Pearson Education.

Illustrations by Sheila Bailey

ISBN: 0-328-13194-6

3 4 5 6 7 8 9 10 V010 14 13 12 11 10 09 08 07 06 05

In the winter, most trees are bare.

But in the spring, their leaves grow back.
Soon the leaves will be green again.

Seasons come and go.
People change their ways.
Animals and plants change too.
Do you remember how?

Spring Rose, Winter Bear

by Dale Cooper
illustrated by Sheila Bailey

PEARSON Scott Foresman

Editorial Offices: Glenview, Illinois • Parsippany, New Jersey • New York, New York
Sales Offices: Needham, Massachusetts • Duluth, Georgia • Glenview, Illinois
Coppell, Texas • Sacramento, California • Mesa, Arizona

Vocabulary

before
does
good-bye
oh
right
won't

Word count: 218

Note: The total word count includes words in the running text and headings only. Numerals and words in chapter titles, captions, labels, diagrams, charts, graphs, sidebars, and extra features are not included.

Think and Share

Read Together

1. What happens to a tree in the spring? What happens to a tree in the summer and fall? Copy the chart on your paper and tell what happens.

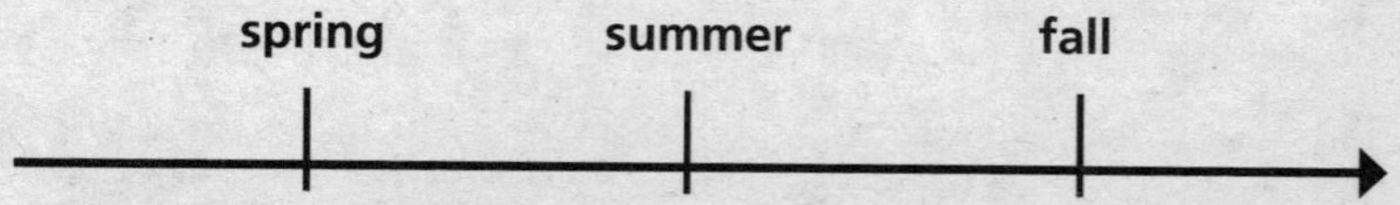

2. What did you know about animals and plants in the winter before you read the book? How did that help you understand what you read?

3. On your own paper, write the two words from this book that end in *-dge* or *-dges*.

4. Turn back to page 6. Look at the pictures, and read the labels. Which two seasons are shown in the pictures?

Suggested levels for Guided Reading, DRA,™ Lexile,® and Reading Recovery™ are provided in the Pearson Scott Foresman Leveling Guide.

Science

Genre	Comprehension Skills and Strategy	Text Features
Expository nonfiction	• Sequence • Compare and Contrast • Prior Knowledge	• Labels

Scott Foresman Reading Street 1.3.6

PEARSON
Scott Foresman

ISBN 0-328-13194-6

9 780328 131945 90000

scottforesman.com

Science

Life Science

Spring Rose, Winter Bear

by Dale Cooper
illustrated by Sheila Bailey

Did you know that a butterfly lays lots of eggs? Caterpillars push out of the eggs.

caterpillar in an egg

Did you know that most caterpillars eat their eggshells? Many caterpillars also eat plants.

Did you know that a caterpillar grows and grows? When it's done, it begins to change.

Did you know that a butterfly greenhouse has flowers? A butterfly drinks nectar from flowers.

Did you know that you can visit their indoor home? It's called a butterfly greenhouse.

First, a caterpillar makes a chrysalis. A chrysalis is like a hard shell. The caterpillar is inside.

chrysalis

In the chrysalis, the caterpillar turns into a pupa. Then the pupa turns into a butterfly. It breaks out of the chrysalis. It will wait and get ready to fly.

Did you know that some butterflies have an indoor home?

Every effort has been made to secure permission and provide appropriate credit for photographic material. The publisher deeply regrets any omission and pledges to correct errors called to its attention in subsequent editions.

Unless otherwise acknowledged, all photographs are the property of Scott Foresman, a division of Pearson Education.

Photo locators denoted as follows: Top (T), Center (C), Bottom (B), Left (L), Right (R), Background (Bkgd)

Opener (TR) DK Images, Opener (B) Digital Vision, Opener (C) DK Images; 1 DK Images; 3 (TR) DK Images, 3 (B) DK Images; 4 Rubberball Productions; 5 Getty Images; 6 (Bkgd) DK Images, 6 (B) DK Images; 7 DK Images; 9 DK Images; 10 (B) DK Images, 10 (T) DK Images; 11 Getty Images; 12 (B) Digital Vision, 12 (T) Digital Vision

ISBN: 0-328-13191-1

3 4 5 6 7 8 9 10 V010 14 13 12 11 10 09 08 07 06 05

Did you know that a butterfly greenhouse is an exciting place? You can watch a caterpillar turn into a butterfly.

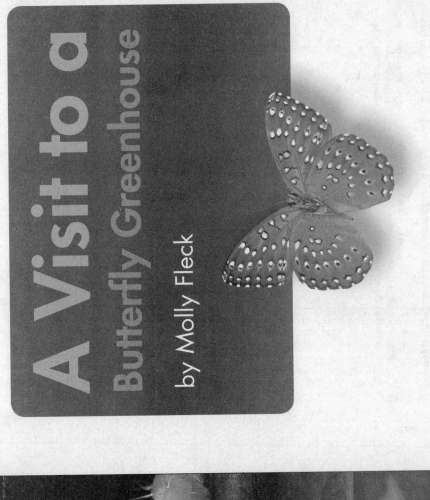

Did you know that people learn a lot
at a butterfly greenhouse?
What did you learn there?

A Visit to a Butterfly Greenhouse

by Molly Fleck

PEARSON
Scott Foresman

Editorial Offices: Glenview, Illinois • Parsippany, New Jersey • New York, New York
Sales Offices: Needham, Massachusetts • Duluth, Georgia • Glenview, Illinois
Coppell, Texas • Sacramento, California • Mesa, Arizona

Vocabulary

done

know

push

visit

wait

Word count: 170

Note: The total word count includes words in the running text and headings only. Numerals and words in chapter titles, captions, labels, diagrams, charts, graphs, sidebars, and extra features are not included.

Think and Share

Read Together

1. Why do people keep some butterflies in a butterfly greenhouse?

2. Copy this chart on your own paper. Write the page number that has information about these stages of the butterfly life cycle.

Page	Life Cycle Stage
	egg
	butterfly

3. Find a contraction on pages 4 and 8. Write the two words that make up the contraction.

4. Look at page 9. What does the picture show you about the chrysalis?

Suggested levels for Guided Reading, DRA™, Lexile,® and Reading Recovery™ are provided in the Pearson Scott Foresman Leveling Guide.

Science

Genre	Comprehension Skills and Strategy	Text Features
Nonfiction	• Draw Conclusions • Author's Purpose • Text Structure	• Labels

Scott Foresman Reading Street 1.3.5

ISBN 0-328-13191-1

9 780328 131914 90000

PEARSON Scott Foresman

scottforesman.com

Science

Life Science

A Visit to a Butterfly Greenhouse

by Molly Fleck

"I'm going to plant my bells," said Jane.

"I'm going to plant some shoes," said Marc.

"You have picked some funny things to plant," said Miss Jones. "But we can try."

The next day, the class went outside.

"We can make the garden here," said Miss Jones.

Soon the class was busy digging. They dug holes in the hard dirt. They planted the zebra and the trumpet and the bells and the shoes.

"What will you plant, Lin?" asked Miss Jones.

"I'll plant my trumpet," said Lin.

Miss Jones smiled again. "I'm afraid that will not grow. But we can try."

"What will you plant, Tom?" asked Miss Jones.

"I'll plant my zebra," said Tom.

Miss Jones smiled. "I'm afraid that will not grow. But we can try."

In a few weeks, things started to grow.

Miss Jones looked out at the yard. "Oh, my! Class, come and see the garden!" she said.

The class ran into the yard.
"Look at my zebra grass!" shouted Tom.
"Here is my trumpet vine!" yelled Lin.
"See my bell flowers?" asked Jane.
"I have a shoe tree!" shouted Marc.

One day Miss Jones read a book about plants and gardens to her class.

"Can we plant a silly garden?" asked Tom.

"Yes!" said Miss Jones. "We can!"

Every effort has been made to secure permission and provide appropriate credit for photographic material. The publisher deeply regrets any omission and pledges to correct errors called to its attention in subsequent editions.

Unless otherwise acknowledged, all photographs are the property of Scott Foresman, a division of Pearson Education.

Photo locators denoted as follows: Top (T), Center (C), Bottom (B), Left (L), Right (R), Background (Bkgd)

Illustrations by Luciana Navarro Alves

ISBN: 0-328-13188-1

2 3 4 5 6 7 8 9 10 V010 14 13 12 11 10 09 08 07 06 05

Miss Jones looked at the garden.

"How did these plants grow?" she asked. "Class, you have planted a funny garden!"

How a Plant Grows

Read Together

A plant starts out as a tiny seed. The seed is planted in soil. The seed needs water and sunlight to grow. Soon the seed will grow roots below the ground. A stem will push up through the soil. As the stem grows taller, leaves will appear. The plant may grow flowers too. Inside each flower new seeds grow. These seeds might make new plants.

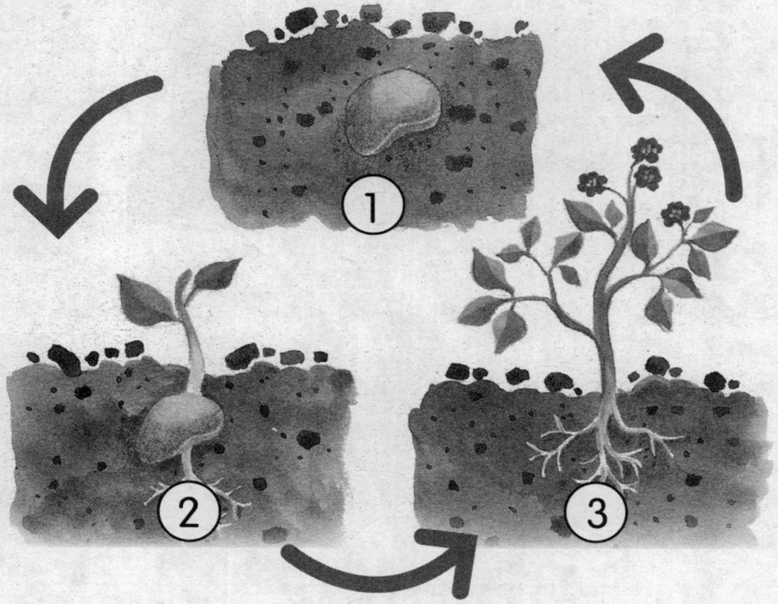

A Funny Garden

by Rowan Obach

illustrated by
Luciana Navarro Alves

PEARSON
Scott Foresman

Editorial Offices: Glenview, Illinois • Parsippany, New Jersey • New York, New York
Sales Offices: Needham, Massachusetts • Duluth, Georgia • Glenview, Illinois
Coppell, Texas • Ontario, California • Mesa, Arizona

Vocabulary

afraid
again
few
how
read
soon

Word count: 234

Note: The total word count includes words in the running text and headings only. Numerals and words in chapter titles, captions, labels, diagrams, charts, graphs, sidebars, and extra features are not included.

Think and Share

Read Together

1. Tell what happened in the beginning, the middle, and at the end of this story. Use a chart like the one below.

Beginning
↓
Middle
↓
End

2. What pictures did you have in your mind as you read this story? How did they help you understand what you were reading?

3. On your own paper, write all the words in this book that have the vowel sound you hear in *jar*.

4. What funny thing would you plant in the garden? What kind of plant would you hope to grow?

Suggested levels for Guided Reading, DRA,™ Lexile,® and Reading Recovery™ are provided in the Pearson Scott Foresman Leveling Guide.

Genre	Comprehension Skills and Strategy
Fantasy	• Plot • Setting • Visualize

Scott Foresman Reading Street 1.3.4

ISBN 0-328-13188-1

9 780328 131884 90000

PEARSON
Scott Foresman

scottforesman.com

A Funny Garden

by Rowan Obach

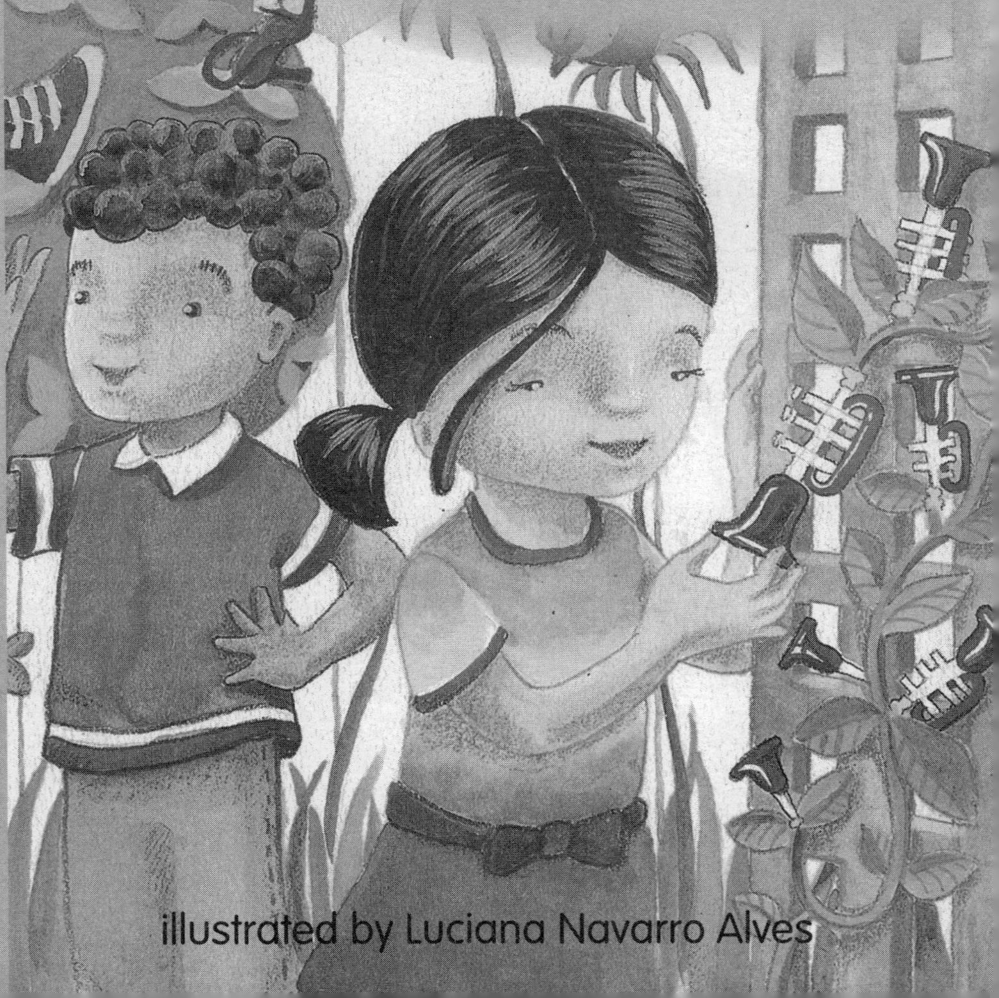

illustrated by Luciana Navarro Alves

"Why do we need a park?" a neighbor named Ed asked at the meeting.

"We could play sports in a park," Norm said.

"We could sit under trees in a park," Pam said.

"We could take walks in a park," Ted said.

"We could feed ducks in a park," Mom said.

"What do you think, Ed? Do you see why we need a park?" Dad asked.

"Yes, I sure do see why we need one," Ed said.

"We need a neighborhood park," Norm said.

"That is a very good idea," Dad said. "We can see if other people think so too. We can have a meeting."

"We can drive our car or ride buses to get around," Mom said.

"We have everything we need here," Dad said.

"We do not have everything we need," Norm said.

"Let's all help make the park. We can plant patches of grass. We can plant flowers and bushes and trees," Mom said.

Everyone helped. Some people cut away weeds and thorns. Some people planted seeds and trees. Some people made paths. Some people made a place for sports.

Mom, Dad, and Norm left their house to take a walk in the neighborhood. They waved to their friends.

"I like our neighborhood," Dad said. "We have a school. We have stores. We have places to eat."

Every effort has been made to secure permission and provide appropriate credit for photographic material. The publisher deeply regrets any omission and pledges to correct errors called to its attention in subsequent editions.

Unless otherwise acknowledged, all photographs are the property of Scott Foresman, a division of Pearson Education.

Photo locators denoted as follows: Top (T), Center (C), Bottom (B), Left (L), Right (R), Background (Bkgd)

Illustrations by Martin Lemelman

Photograph 12 Library of Congress

ISBN: 0-328-13185-7

2 3 4 5 6 7 8 9 10 V010 14 13 12 11 10 09 08 07 06 05

At last the park was done. There were paths. There were benches and trees. There was a place for sports. There was a pond for ducks.

"Now our neighorhood has everything we need!" Norm said.

The One-Room Schoolhouse

Read Together

Communities change over time. Important parts of communities change too. Schools are important parts of communities. Schools are very different today from schools long ago. Most schools today have separate classrooms for different grades. There is a teacher for each class. But in the past some schools were in buildings with only one room. These schools had only one teacher for all the grades. What is your school like?

The New Park

by Ellen Leigh
illustrated by Martin Lemelman

PEARSON
Scott Foresman

Editorial Offices: Glenview, Illinois • Parsippany, New Jersey • New York, New York
Sales Offices: Needham, Massachusetts • Duluth, Georgia • Glenview, Illinois
Coppell, Texas • Ontario, California • Mesa, Arizona

Vocabulary

away

car

friends

house

our

school

very

Word count: 256

Note: The total word count includes words in the running text and headings only. Numerals and words in chapter titles, captions, labels, diagrams, charts, graphs, sidebars, and extra features are not included.

Think and Share

Read Together

1. What is the big idea of this story?
2. What kinds of things did people plan to do in the park? Show them on a web like this one.

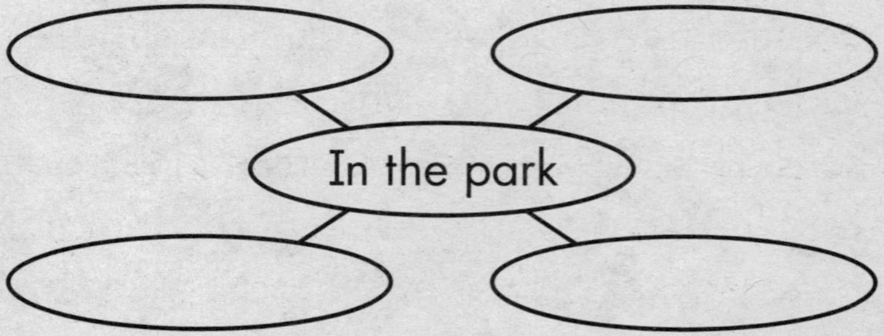

3. Find words in this story that have the *-or* sound that you hear in the word *thorn*. Make a list.
4. Do you think Norm had a good idea for a change in his neighborhood? What change would you like to make in your neighborhood?

Suggested levels for Guided Reading, DRA™, Lexile,® and Reading Recovery™ are provided in the Pearson Scott Foresman Leveling Guide.

Genre	Comprehension Skills and Strategy
Realistic fiction	• Theme • Setting • Monitor and Fix Up

Scott Foresman Reading Street 1.3.3

ISBN 0-328-13185-7

PEARSON
Scott Foresman
scottforesman.com

The New Park

by Ellen Leigh illustrated by Martin Lemelman

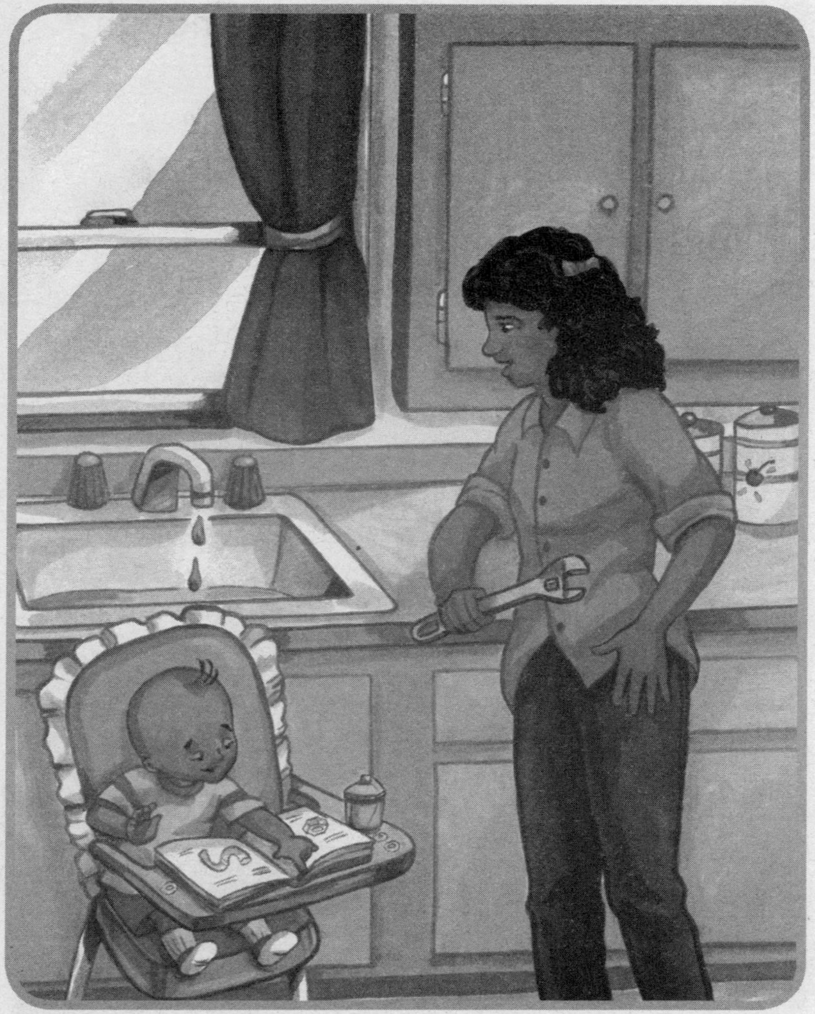

Mac was not just any boy.
At three weeks old, he could fix things!
"Will we ever fix this sink?" said Mom.
"I will fix it!" said Mac.

"Are you sure you are old enough?" said Mom.

"Yes, I can do it on my own," said Mac.

And Mac fixed the sink!

Mac was not just any boy.
At four weeks old, he could read numbers!

"Our mailman is sick today," said Dad.

"I will do his job," said Mac.

"Are you sure you are old enough?" said Dad.

"Yes, I can do it on my own," said Mac.

And Mac won the race!

Mac was not just any boy.
At two weeks old, he could run!
"There is a race outside," said Dad.
"I will run past everyone," said Mac.

"Are you sure you are old enough?" said Dad.

"Yes, I can read the mailbox numbers on my own," said Mac.

And Mac gave out the mail!

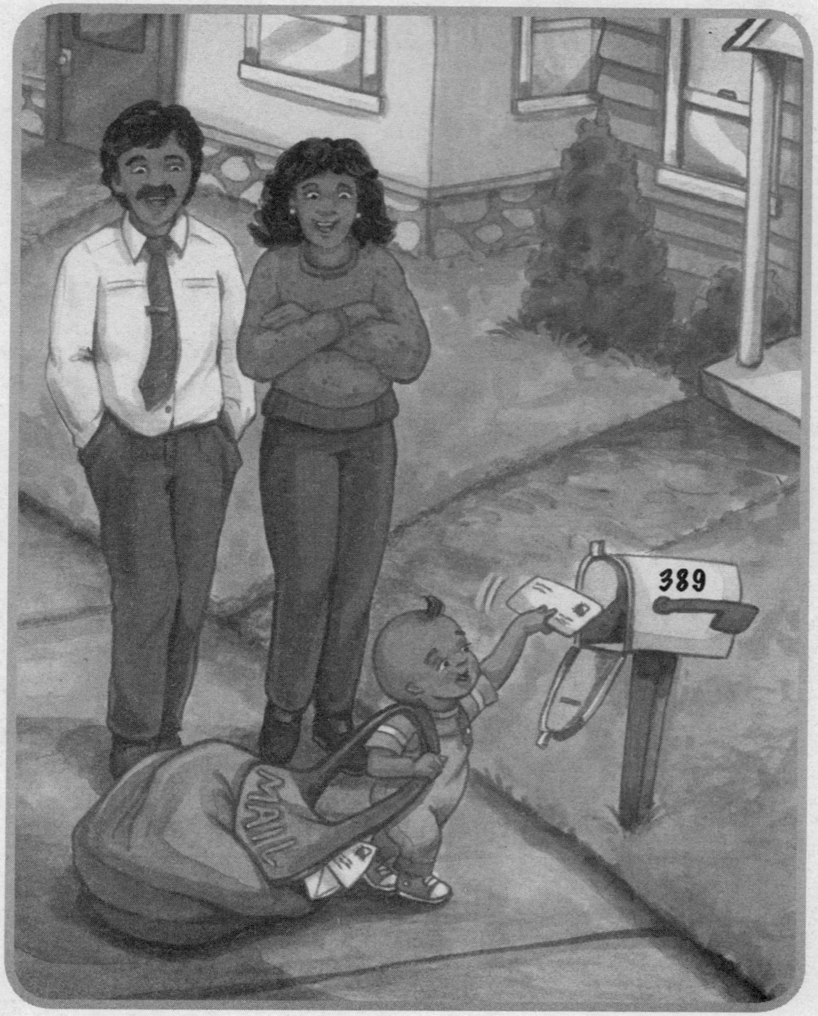

Mac was not just any boy.
At five weeks old, he flew a spaceship!
Mom and Dad were watching.
"Will you go to the moon?" they said.

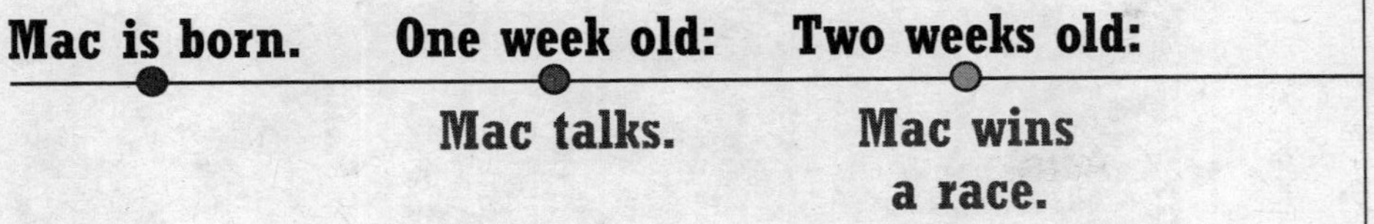

Once there was a family.
They had a baby boy.
Mac was not just any boy.
At one week old, he could talk.

Every effort has been made to secure permission and provide appropriate credit for photographic material. The publisher deeply regrets any omission and pledges to correct errors called to its attention in subsequent editions.

Unless otherwise acknowledged, all photographs are the property of Scott Foresman, a division of Pearson Education.

Photo locators denoted as follows: Top (T), Center (C), Bottom (B), Left (L), Right (R), Background (Bkgd)

Illustrations by Linda Howard Bittner

Photograph 12 Digital Vision

ISBN: 0-328-13182-2

3 4 5 6 7 8 9 10 V010 14 13 12 11 10 09 08 07 06 05

"Yes, I can fly there on my own," said Mac.

And he did.

Three weeks old:	Four weeks old:	Five weeks old:
Mac fixes the sink.	Mac gives out the mail.	Mac flies a spaceship.

Read Together

Different Ways To Grow

A human baby does not walk until the baby is around one year old. But many animals walk sooner than that. A baby elephant learns to stand as soon as it is born. A baby reindeer must run to keep up with the herd. It runs soon after birth.

Most baby birds spend their first few weeks in the nest. Then they learn to fly so that they can find food. As soon as baby dolphins are born, they swim to the surface. They need to take their first breath.

Every living thing grows differently.

Not Just Any Boy

by Dale Cooper

illustrated by Linda Howard Bittner

PEARSON
Scott Foresman

Editorial Offices: Glenview, Illinois • Parsippany, New Jersey • New York, New York
Sales Offices: Needham, Massachusetts • Duluth, Georgia • Glenview, Illinois
Coppell, Texas • Sacramento, California • Mesa, Arizona

Vocabulary

any

enough

ever

every

own

sure

were

Word count: 221

Note: The total word count includes words in the running text and headings only. Numerals and words in chapter titles, captions, labels, diagrams, charts, graphs, sidebars, and extra features are not included.

Think and Share

Read Together

1. What did Mac do at the beginning of this story? What did Mac do in the middle? What did he do at the end?
2. Tell the main things that happened in this story.
3. Find the compound words on pages 8 and 9. Write the two words that make up each compound word. Circle the word both compound words share.
4. Create a time line of your life using the guide below. Include some things you have done at different ages. Ask someone at home for help.

I have learned how to:

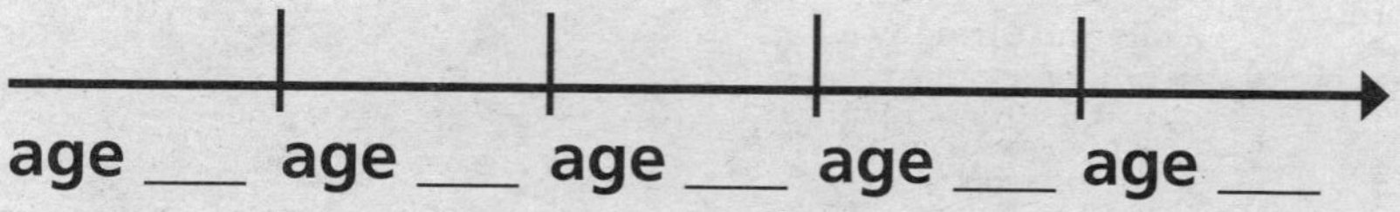

Suggested levels for Guided Reading, DRA,™ Lexile,® and Reading Recovery™ are provided in the Pearson Scott Foresman Leveling Guide.

Genre	Comprehension Skills and Strategy
Fantasy	• Plot • Realism and Fantasy • Summarize

Scott Foresman Reading Street 1.3.2

PEARSON
Scott Foresman
scottforesman.com

ISBN 0-328-13182-2

Not Just Any Boy

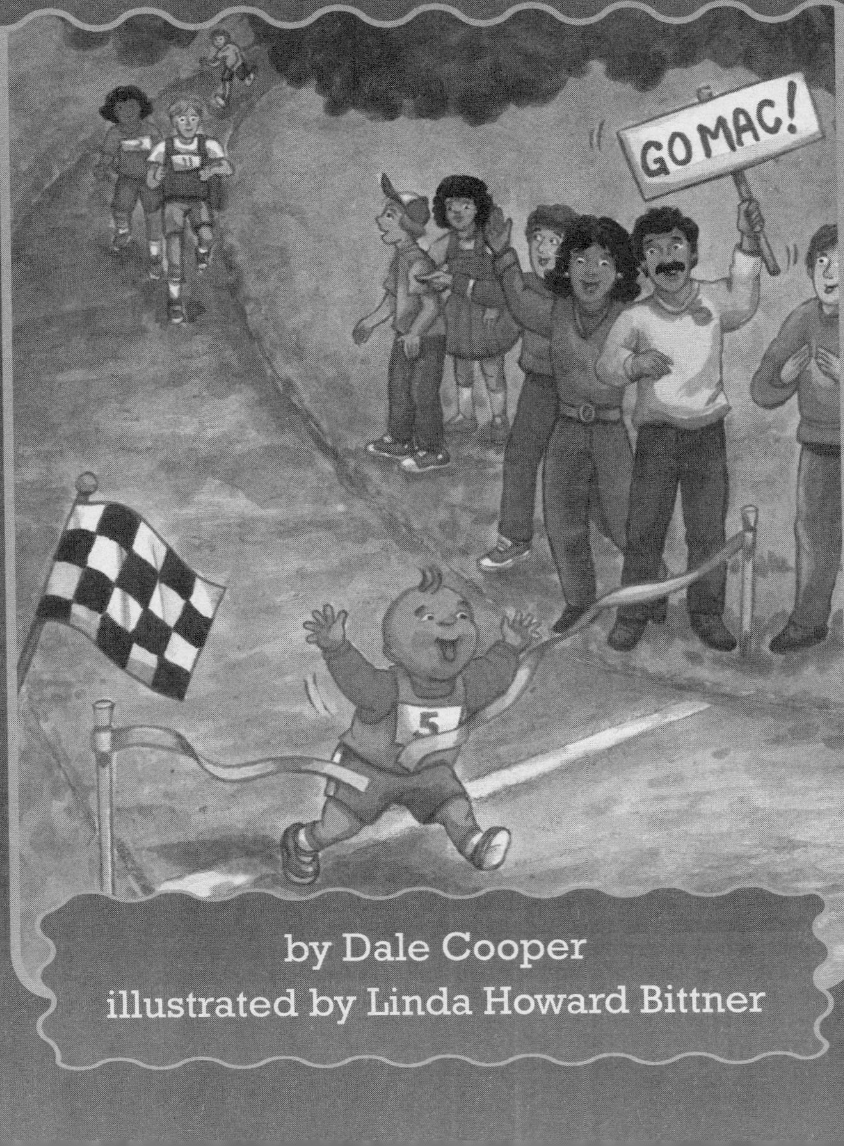

by Dale Cooper

illustrated by Linda Howard Bittner

The baby is nothing like me.

He is so small!

And he likes to cry all day!

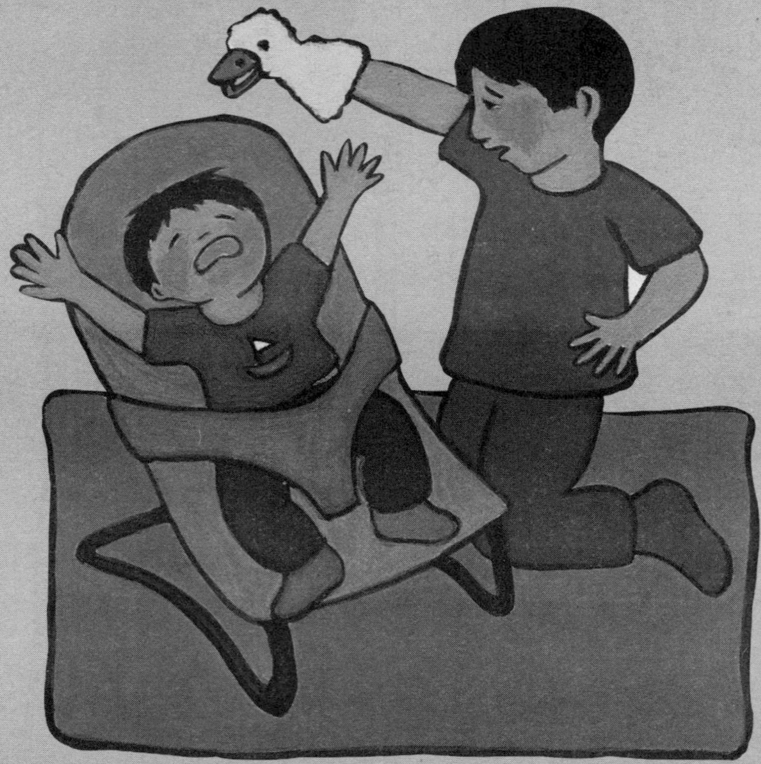

His feet are little.

Mine are big!

His eyes are blue.

Mine are not blue.

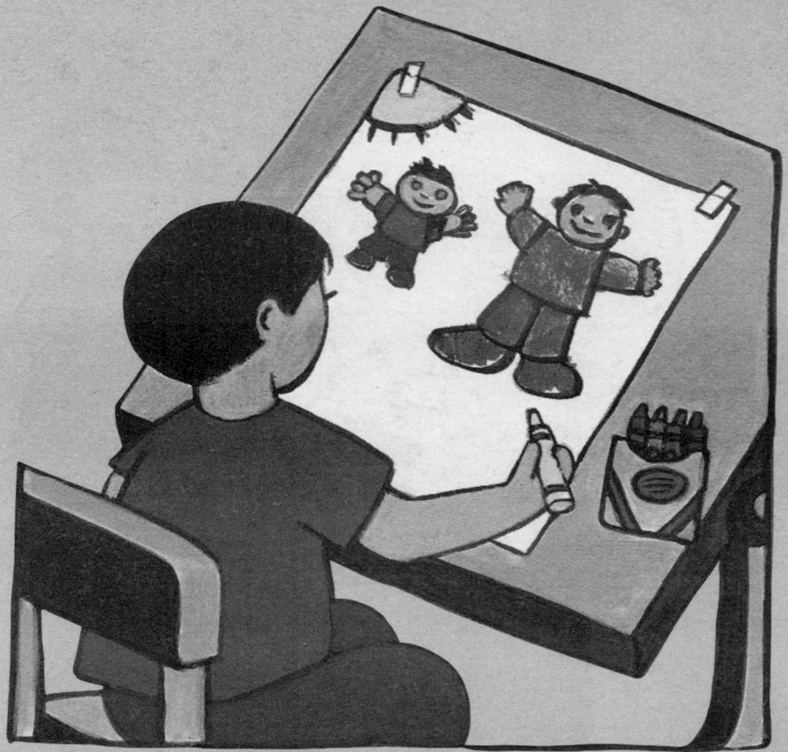

But he has black hair.

And my hair is black.

His nose looks a little like mine too.

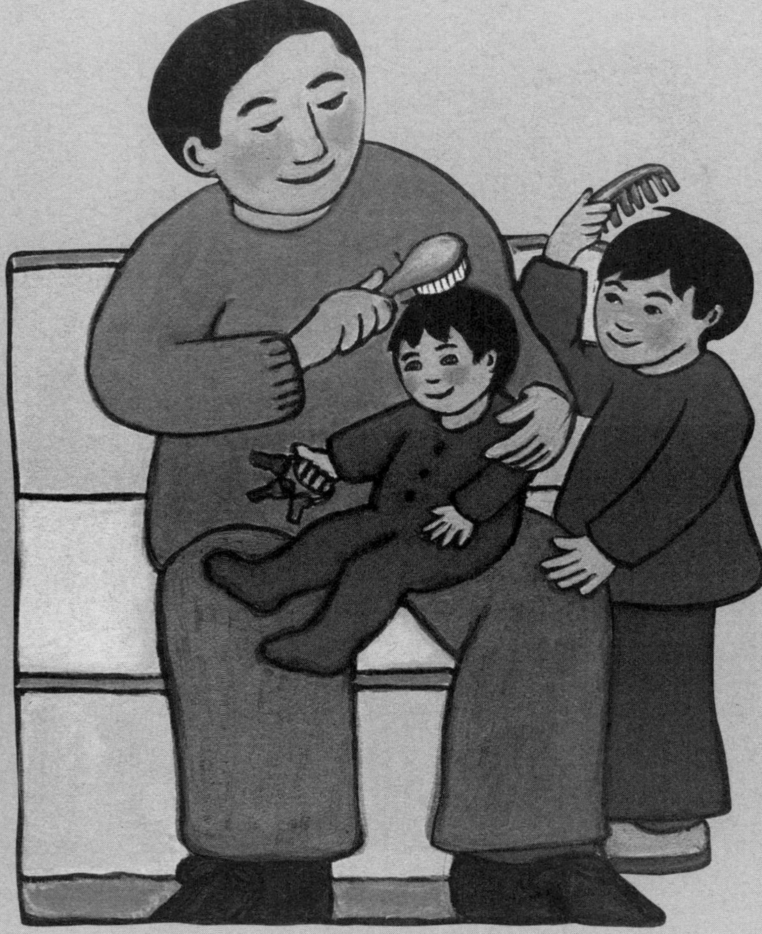

Look at the baby.

The other day, my dad said the baby
looks just like me.

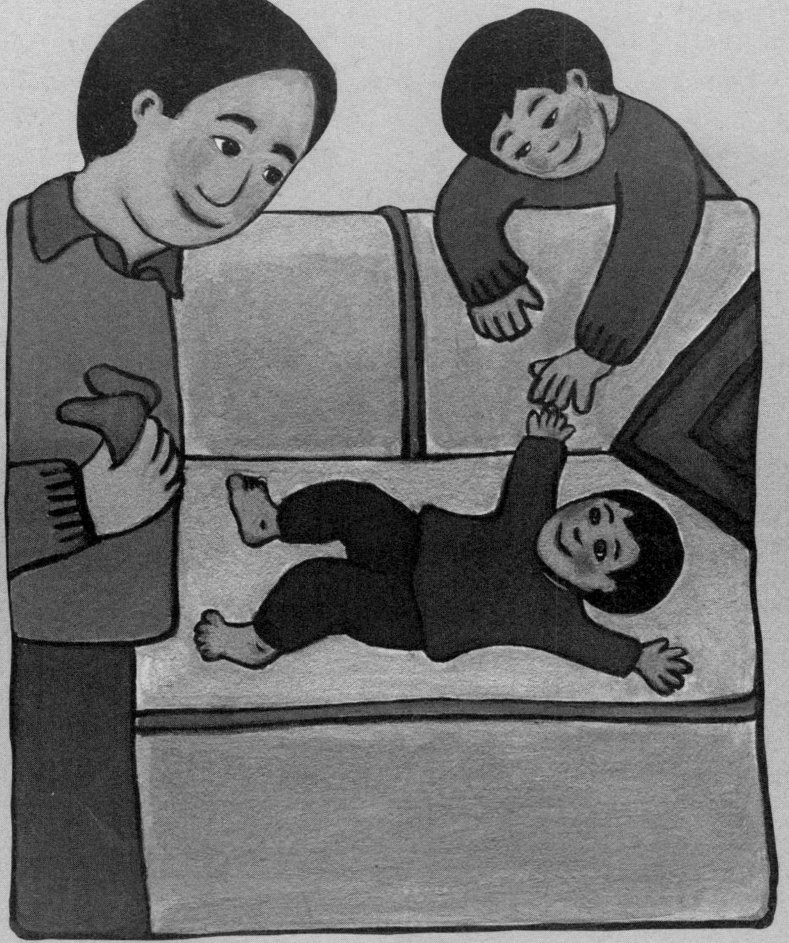

Every effort has been made to secure permission and provide appropriate credit for photographic material. The publisher deeply regrets any omission and pledges to correct errors called to its attention in subsequent editions.

Unless otherwise acknowledged, all photographs are the property of Scott Foresman, a division of Pearson Education.

Photo locators denoted as follows: Top (T), Center (C), Bottom (B), Left (L), Right (R), Background (Bkgd)

Illustrations by Freddie Levin

ISBN: 0-328-13179-2

2 3 4 5 6 7 8 9 10 V010 14 13 12 11 10 09 08 07 06 05

He has the same smile as I do.

Not everything about him is like me.

But I see a lot of things that are.

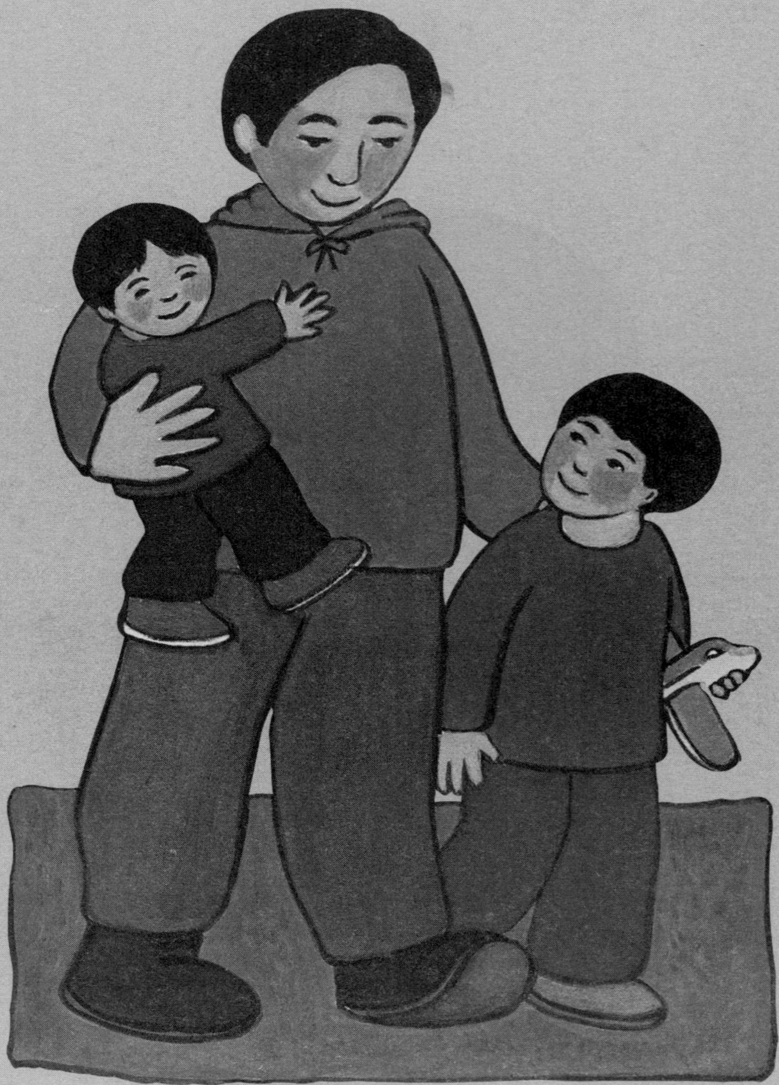

I like that we are almost the same!

I hope it always stays this way.

Will we become tall like Dad?

I hope we do!

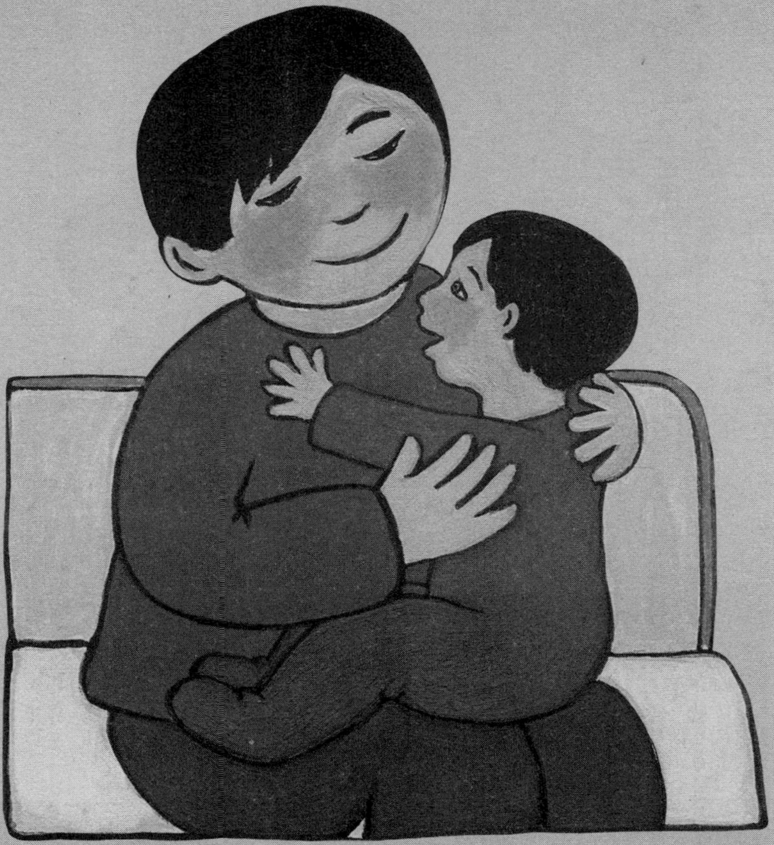

Just Like Me

by Mary Katherine Tate

illustrated by Freddie Levin

PEARSON Scott Foresman

Editorial Offices: Glenview, Illinois • Parsippany, New Jersey • New York, New York
Sales Offices: Needham, Massachusetts • Duluth, Georgia • Glenview, Illinois
Coppell, Texas • Ontario, California • Mesa, Arizona

Vocabulary

always
become
day
everything
nothing
stays
things

Word count: 115

Note: The total word count includes words in the running text and headings only. Numerals and words in chapter titles, captions, labels, diagrams, charts, graphs, sidebars, and extra features are not included.

Think and Share

Read Together

1. How does the boy think the baby is like him? How does he think he and the baby are different? Copy the chart on your paper and write how they are the same and how they are different.

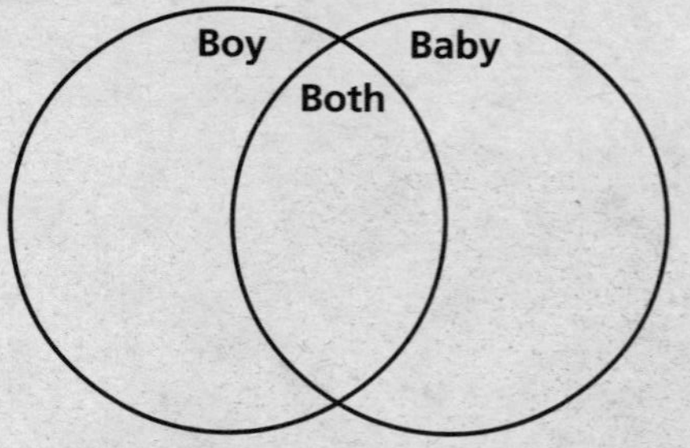

2. How do you think the boy will feel if the baby grows up to look a lot like him? Why do you think this?

3. On a piece of paper, write all the words from the book that have the word *thing* as part of a bigger word.

4. How does the picture on page 8 show how the boy feels about his brother?

Suggested levels for Guided Reading, DRA™, Lexile,® and Reading Recovery™ are provided in the Pearson Scott Foresman Leveling Guide.

Science

Genre	Comprehension Skills and Strategy
Narrative nonfiction	• Compare and Contrast • Draw Conclusions • Predict

Scott Foresman Reading Street 1.3.1

ISBN 0-328-13179-2

PEARSON
Scott Foresman

scottforesman.com

Science

Just Like Me

by Mary Katherine Tate

illustrated by Freddie Levin

We use honey in many ways.

We can eat honey.

It is sweet and good!

We can take honey on a picnic.

We can use honey to cook.

We can use it to make bread.

We can also use it to make cakes.

We can use honey when we are sick.

It may help us feel good.

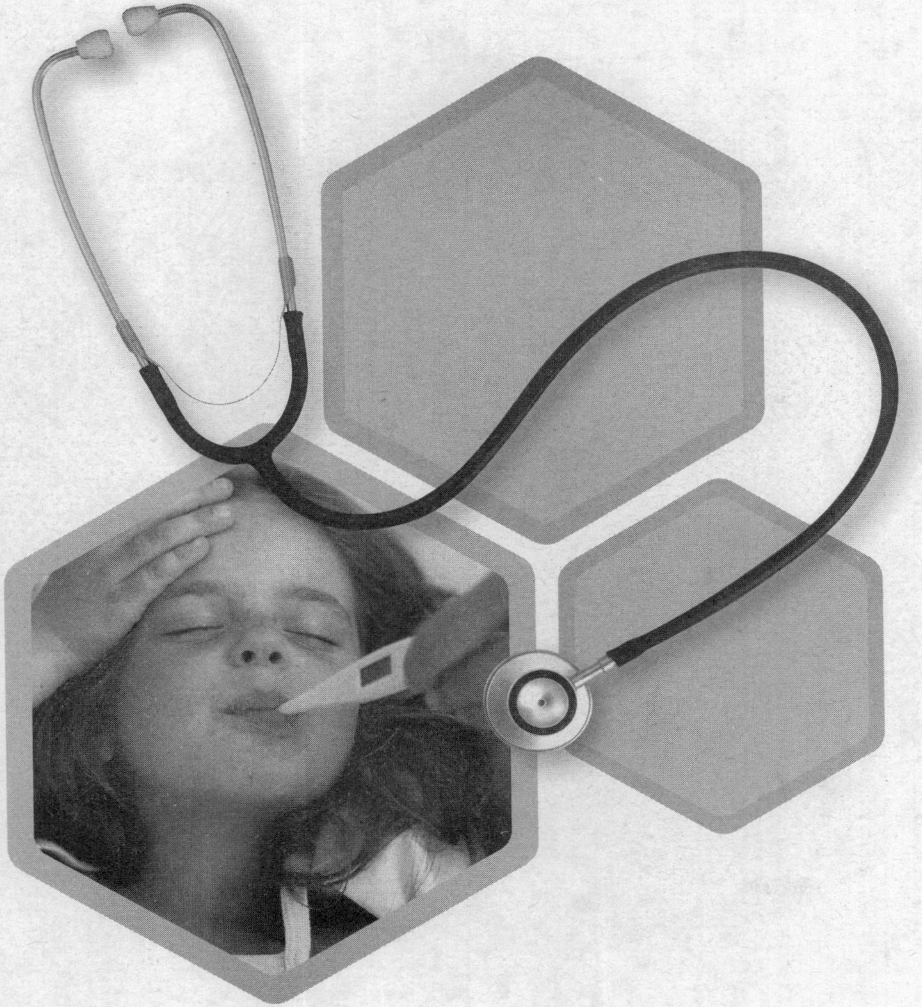

Some people keep bees.

Bees do many jobs.

They make sweet honey in their hives.

Every effort has been made to secure permission and provide appropriate credit for photographic material. The publisher deeply regrets any omission and pledges to correct errors called to its attention in subsequent editions.

Unless otherwise acknowledged, all photographs are the property of Scott Foresman, a division of Pearson Education.

Photo locators denoted as follows: Top (T), Center (C), Bottom (B), Left (L), Right (R), Background (Bkgd)

Opener (C) Digital Vision, (C) ©Comstock, Inc.; 1 (C) Brand X Pictures; 3 (C) Digital Vision; (BC) Brand X Pictures; 4 (C) ©Comstock, Inc., (BR) Brand X Pictures; 5 (T) ©Stockbyte, (BC) ©Comstock, Inc.; 6 (C) Brand X Pictures, (BL) Image Source; 7 (T) ©Image Source Limited, (BR) ©Comstock Inc.; 8 (CL) Brand X Pictures, (TR) Getty Images

ISBN: 0-328-13176-8

3 4 5 6 7 8 9 10 V010 14 13 12 11 10 09 08 07 06 05

We can put honey in the tub.

We can mix honey with the water.

The honey can make our skin soft.

Bees make sweet honey.

We use it in many ways.

What are the ways your family uses honey?

Think of some other new ways to use it.

We Use Honey

by Zachary Cohn

PEARSON
Scott Foresman

Editorial Offices: Glenview, Illinois • Parsippany, New Jersey • New York, New York
Sales Offices: Needham, Massachusetts • Duluth, Georgia • Glenview, Illinois
Coppell, Texas • Sacramento, California • Mesa, Arizona

Vocabulary

also
family
new
other
some
their

Word count: 120

Note: The total word count includes words in the running text and headings only. Numerals and words in chapter titles, captions, labels, diagrams, charts, graphs, sidebars, and extra features are not included.

Think and Share

Read Together

1. How is honey like sugar? How is honey different from sugar? Copy the chart and write your answers.

Honey	Sugar

2. What clues did the cover give you about this book?
3. Write the word *picnic* on your paper. Under each letter, write whether it is a vowel (v) or a consonant (c). How did this pattern help you read the word?
4. What do the pictures on pages 4 and 5 show you about honey?

Suggested levels for Guided Reading, DRA,™ Lexile,® and Reading Recovery™ are provided in the Pearson Scott Foresman Leveling Guide.

Science

Genre	Comprehension Skills and Strategy
Nonfiction	• Compare and Contrast • Draw Conclusions • Preview

Scott Foresman Reading Street 1.2.6

PEARSON
Scott Foresman
scottforesman.com

ISBN 0-328-13176-8
9 780328 131761 90000

Science

Life Science

We Use Honey

by Zachary Cohn

This forest is a good place for trees.

They get the water and the sun they need to grow here.

This forest is a good place for people to play.

They sit around under the trees.

They look at birds and animals.

They paddle on the lake.

These people do not take care of the forest.

They cut down huge trees.

They drop trash on the ground.

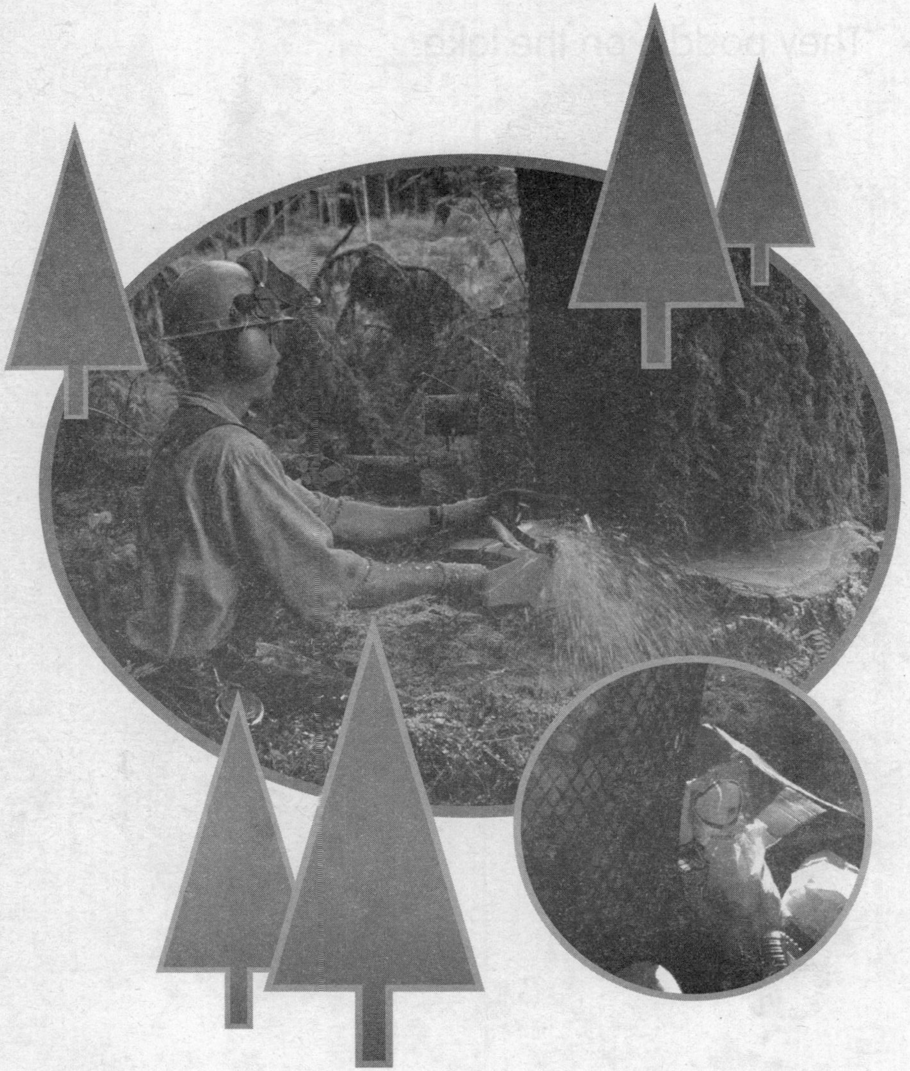

This forest is a good place for animals and birds.

They can find food and make homes here.

Every effort has been made to secure permission and provide appropriate credit for photographic material. The publisher deeply regrets any omission and pledges to correct errors called to its attention in subsequent editions.

Unless otherwise acknowledged, all photographs are the property of Scott Foresman, a division of Pearson Education.

Photo locators denoted as follows: Top (T), Center (C), Bottom (B), Left (L), Right (R), Background (Bkgd)

Opener (C) Digital Vision, Opener (Bkgd) Digital Vision; 1 (C) Digital Vision; 3 (C) Digital Vision, 3 (T) Getty Images, 3 (BL) Brand X Pictures; 4 (TL) © Dorling Kindersley, 4 (C) Digital Vision; 5 (C) © Comstock Inc., 5 (BR) Brand X Pictures; 6 (C) Getty Images, 6 (BR) Getty Images; 7 (TL) Getty Images, (C) Getty Images; 8 (C) Digital Vision, 8 (BL) ImageState

ISBN: 0-328-13173-3

3 4 5 6 7 8 9 10 V010 14 13 12 11 10 09 08 07 06 05

The trees are gone.

The birds cannot find homes.

The animals cannot find food.

People must take care of the forest.

They must make it a good home for trees, birds, and animals.

How can you help the forest?

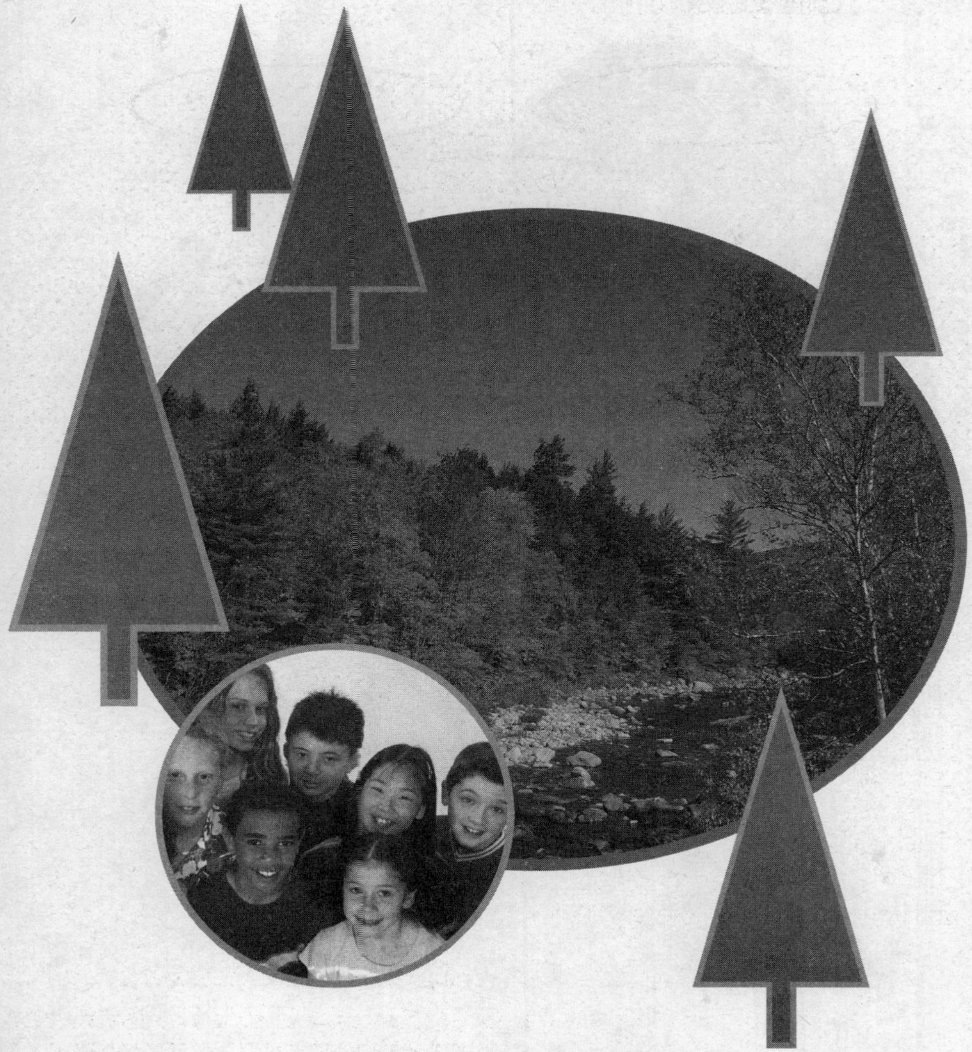

Help the Forest

by Rita Crosby

PEARSON
Scott Foresman

Editorial Offices: Glenview, Illinois • Parsippany, New Jersey • New York, New York
Sales Offices: Needham, Massachusetts • Duluth, Georgia • Glenview, Illinois
Coppell, Texas • Sacramento, California • Mesa, Arizona

Vocabulary

around

find

food

grow

under

water

Word count: 124

Note: The total word count includes words in the running text and headings only. Numerals and words in chapter titles, captions, labels, diagrams, charts, graphs, sidebars, and extra features are not included.

Think and Share

Read Together

1. Why do you think the author wrote about caring for the forest? Make a web like this one and use it for your answers.

2. What clues did the cover give you about this book?
3. What vowel sound do you hear in the word *huge*?
4. What do the pictures on page 6 show you about what some people did to the forest?

Suggested levels for Guided Reading, DRA,™ Lexile,® and Reading Recovery™ are provided in the Pearson Scott Foresman Leveling Guide.

Science

Genre	Comprehension Skills and Strategy
Nonfiction	• Author's Purpose • Cause and Effect • Preview

Scott Foresman Reading Street 1.2.5

PEARSON Scott Foresman

scottforesman.com

ISBN 0-328-13173-3

9 780328 131730 90000

Science

Earth Science

Help the Forest

by Rita Crosby

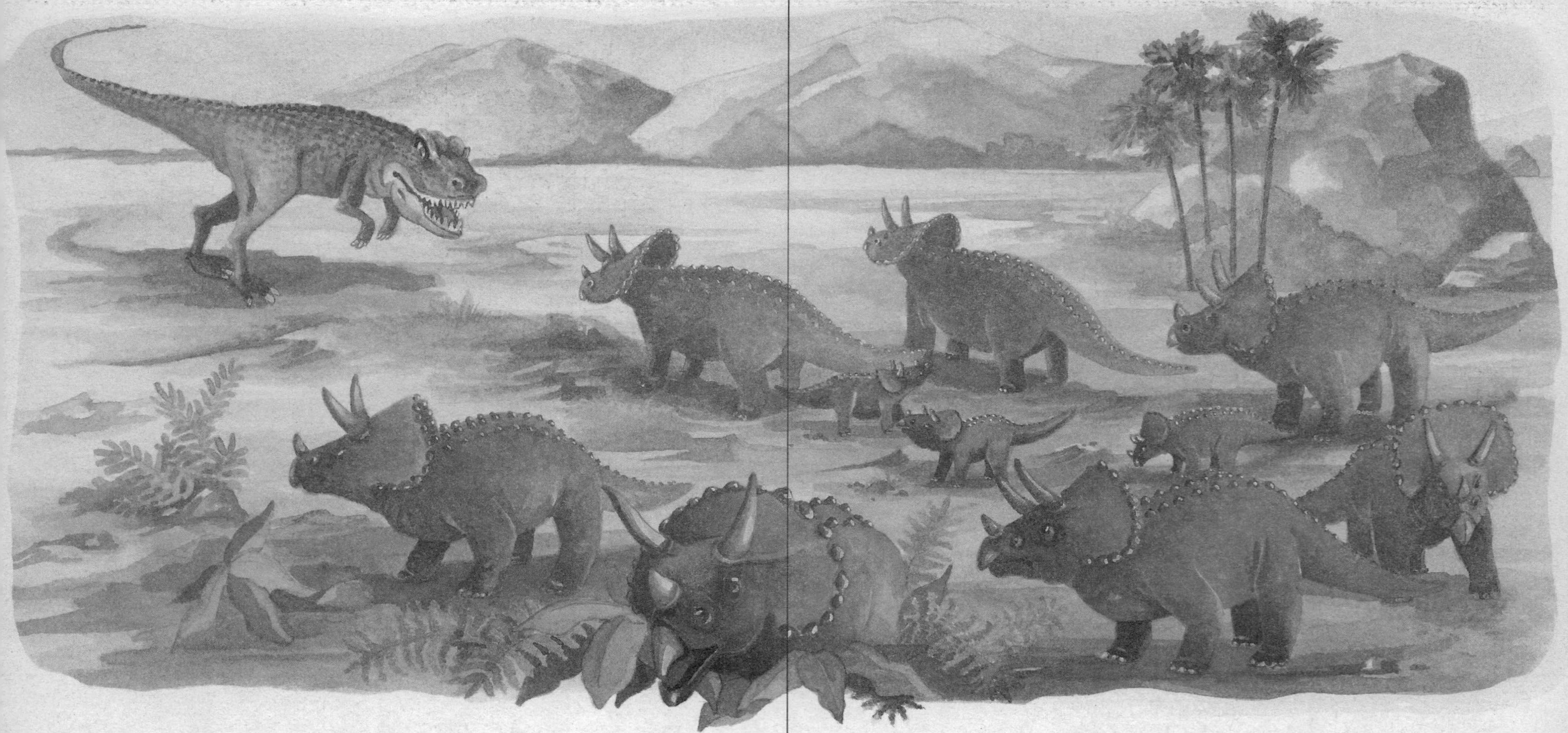

Many dinosaurs did live in herds.
In herds, many animals live together.

Dinosaur herds could work together.
This herd made a circle.
The baby dinosaurs went inside.
There they could be safe.

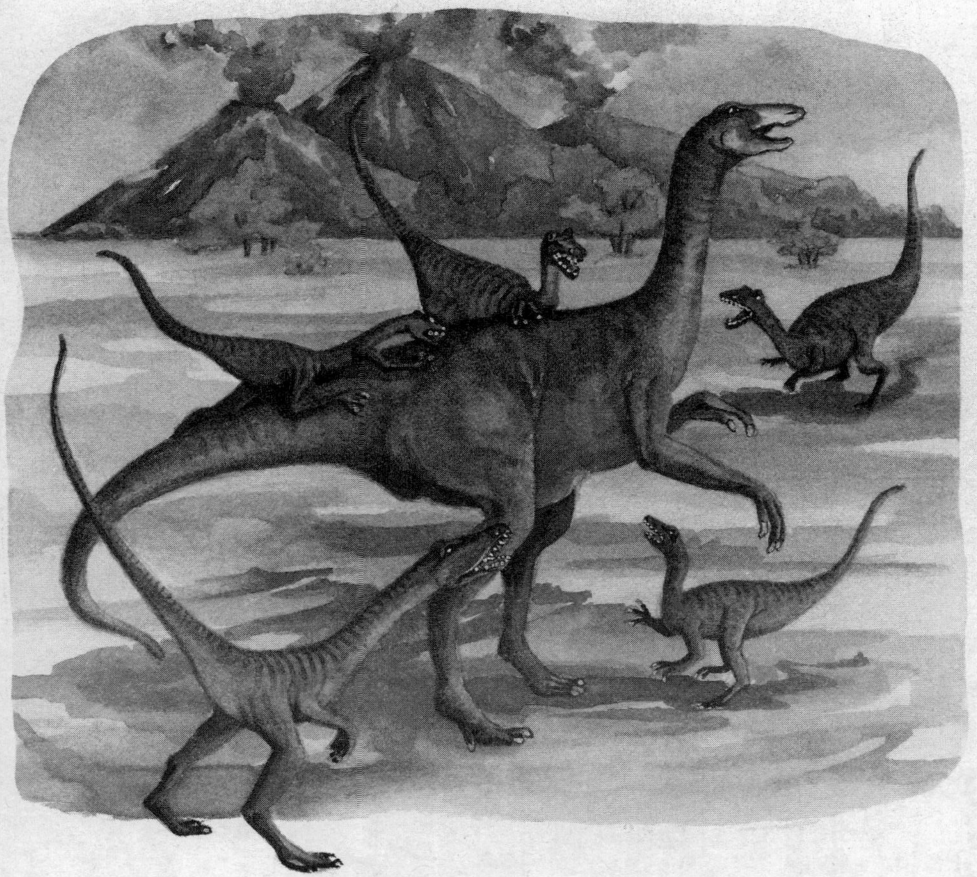

Dinosaur herds could hunt together.
This herd will push the big dinosaur down.
It will be their dinner.

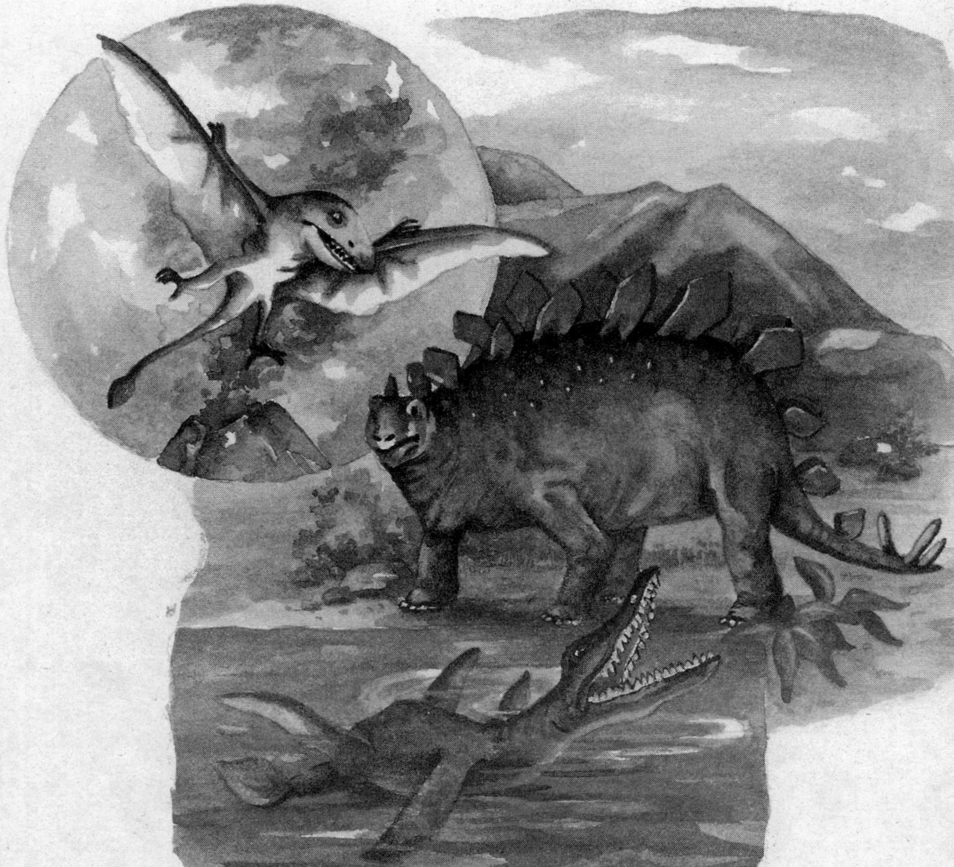

Dinosaurs don't live now.
They did live in the past.
These dinosaurs did live alone.

Every effort has been made to secure permission and provide appropriate credit for photographic material. The publisher deeply regrets any omission and pledges to correct errors called to its attention in subsequent editions.

Unless otherwise acknowledged, all photographs are the property of Scott Foresman, a division of Pearson Education.

Illustrations by Burgandy Beam

ISBN: 0-328-13170-9

3 4 5 6 7 8 9 10 V010 14 13 12 11 10 09 08 07 06 05

Dinosaur herds could make nests together.
This herd made a nest for eggs.
The big dinosaur kept the nest safe.

Dinosaurs don't live now.
They did live in the past.
These dinosaurs did live in herds.

Dinosaur Herds

by Tim Glazer
illustrated by Burgandy Beam

PEARSON Scott Foresman

Editorial Offices: Glenview, Illinois • Parsippany, New Jersey • New York, New York
Sales Offices: Needham, Massachusetts • Duluth, Georgia • Glenview, Illinois
Coppell, Texas • Sacramento, California • Mesa, Arizona

Vocabulary

down

inside

now

there

together

Word count: 101

Note: The total word count includes words in the running text and headings only. Numerals and words in chapter titles, captions, labels, diagrams, charts, graphs, sidebars, and extra features are not included.

Think and Share

Read Together

1. What happens first, next, and last when herds hunt together?

First

↓

Next

↓

Last

2. How did the herd help the baby dinosaurs stay safe? Reread page 5 to check your answer.
3. Find the contraction on page 3.
4. What can you tell about dinosaurs from the picture on page 3?

Suggested levels for Guided Reading, DRA,™ Lexile,® and Reading Recovery™ are provided in the Pearson Scott Foresman Leveling Guide.

Science

Genre	Comprehension Skills and Strategy
Expository nonfiction	• Sequence • Draw Conclusions • Monitor and Fix Up

Scott Foresman Reading Street 1.2.4

ISBN 0-328-13170-9
9 780328 131709 90000

PEARSON
Scott Foresman
scottforesman.com

Life Science

Science

Dinosaur Herds

by Tim Glazer

illustrated by Burgandy Beam

I live in the country.

Look at my neighborhood.

Many farm animals live here.

I live in a city.

Look at my neighborhood.

I have pals who pitch and catch.

I live in a town.

Look at my neighborhood.

I ride my bike with Chad.

I live in a city.

Look at my neighborhood.

Lots of people live and work here.

Every effort has been made to secure permission and provide appropriate credit for photographic material. The publisher deeply regrets any omission and pledges to correct errors called to its attention in subsequent editions.

Unless otherwise acknowledged, all photographs are the property of Scott Foresman, a division of Pearson Education.

Illustrations by Michael Rex

ISBN: 0-328-13167-9

3 4 5 6 7 8 9 10 V010 14 13 12 11 10 09 08 07 06 05

I live at a lake.

Look at my neighborhood.

I swim and go out in boats.

You saw many neighborhoods.

They are not the same.

Which one is like yours?

Neighborhoods

by Barbara L. Luciano
illustrated by Michael Rex

PEARSON
Scott Foresman

Editorial Offices: Glenview, Illinois • Parsippany, New Jersey • New York, New York
Sales Offices: Needham, Massachusetts • Duluth, Georgia • Glenview, Illinois
Coppell, Texas • Sacramento, California • Mesa, Arizona

Vocabulary

live

out

people

who

work

Word count: 91

Note: The total word count includes words in the running text and headings only. Numerals and words in chapter titles, captions, labels, diagrams, charts, graphs, sidebars, and extra features are not included.

Think and Share

Read Together

1. Why does the author write about different neighborhoods?

2. Copy the chart on your paper. Write two questions you have about the book.

My Questions

3. Look at page 5. Which words on this page end in *–tch*?

4. Look at the picture on page 6. What does the picture tell about this neighborhood?

Suggested levels for Guided Reading, DRA™, Lexile,® and Reading Recovery™ are provided in the Pearson Scott Foresman Leveling Guide.

Social Studies

Genre	Comprehension Skills and Strategy
Nonfiction	• Author's Purpose • Compare and Contrast • Ask Questions

Scott Foresman Reading Street 1.2.3

ISBN 0-328-13167-9

PEARSON
Scott Foresman

scottforesman.com

Social Studies

Neighborhoods

by Barbara L. Luciano
illustrated by Michael Rex

The class can work in a group.
They share the pens.
They draw on paper.

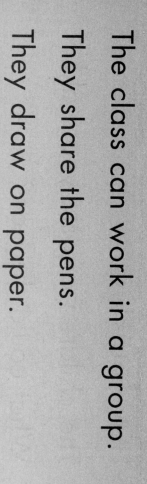

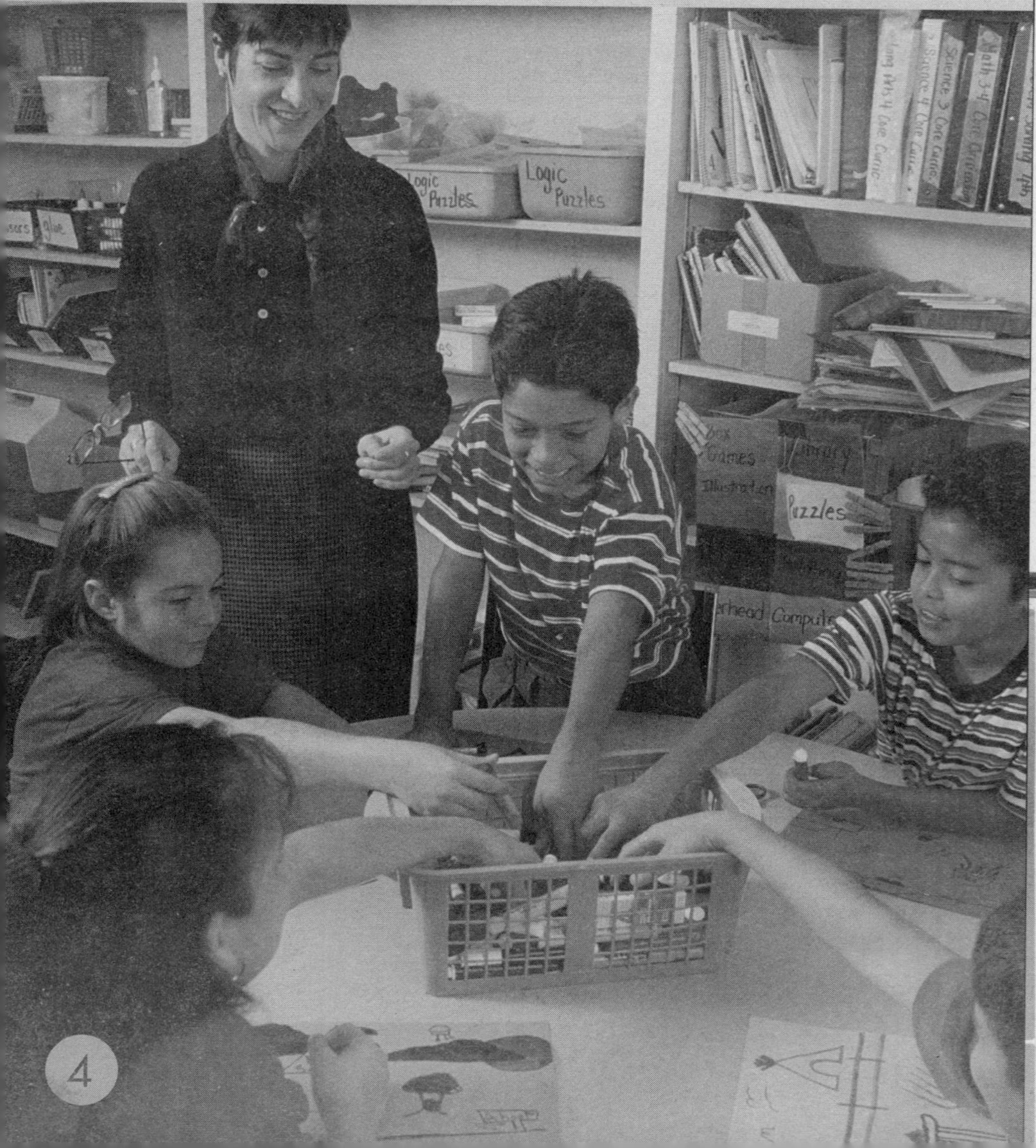

The class has jobs.
They have a pet in a cage.
They take care of their bird.

The class looks at pictures.

They name the animals.

They say, "Horse, pig, duck."

Here is a class.

The children are six years old.

What could they do?

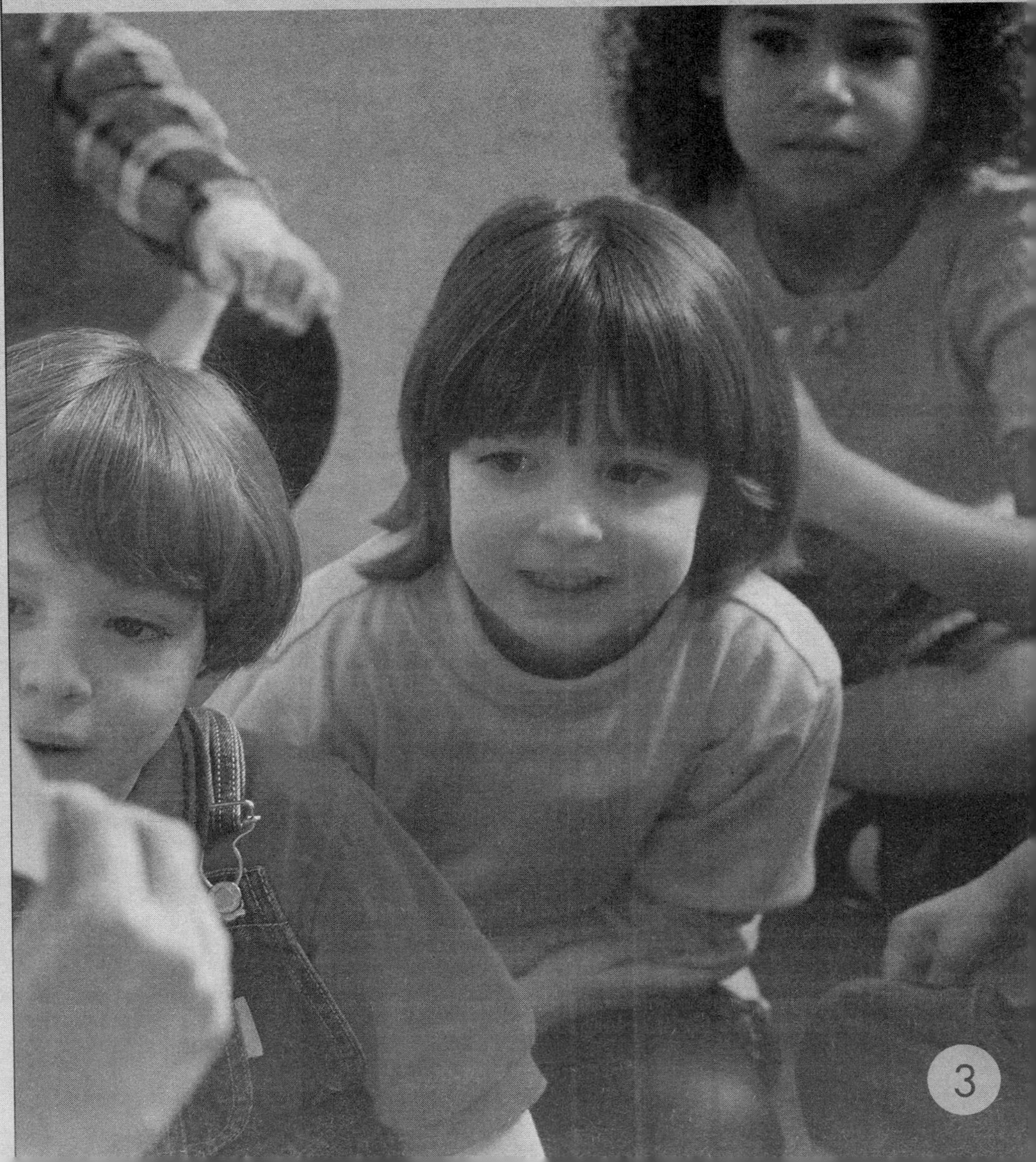

Every effort has been made to secure permission and provide appropriate credit for photographic material. The publisher deeply regrets any omission and pledges to correct errors called to its attention in subsequent editions.

Unless otherwise acknowledged, all photographs are the property of Scott Foresman, a division of Pearson Education.

Photo locators denoted as follows: Top (T), Center (C), Bottom (B), Left (L), Right (R), Background (Bkgd)

Opener Getty Images; 1 Rubberball Productions; 3 Getty Images; 4 (B) DK Images; Getty Images; 5 (CR) © Comstock Inc.; 6 (CR) © DK Images, 6 (TL) © Dorling Kindersley; 6 (B) DK Images; 7 DK Images; 8 Rubberball Productions; 8 (B) Corbis

ISBN: 0-328-13164-4

3 4 5 6 7 8 9 10 V010 14 13 12 11 10 09 08 07 06 05

The class likes to play.
They climb up the ladder.
They go down the slide.

The children take their places
on the bus.
They will be home soon.
Is this class like yours?

The Class

by Beatrice Reynolds

PEARSON Scott Foresman

Editorial Offices: Glenview, Illinois • Parsippany, New Jersey • New York, New York
Sales Offices: Needham, Massachusetts • Duluth, Georgia • Glenview, Illinois
Coppell, Texas • Sacramento, California • Mesa, Arizona

Vocabulary

be
could
horse
old
paper

Word count: 93

Note: The total word count includes words in the running text and headings only. Numerals and words in chapter titles, captions, labels, diagrams, charts, graphs, sidebars, and extra features are not included.

Think and Share

Read Together

1. Reread page 8. Copy the chart on your own paper. Tell why the children get on the bus.

What happened?
The children get on the bus.

↓

Why did it happen?

2. Look at the picture on page 4. How do you know that this picture was taken in a classroom?

3. Find the word on page 5 that has the long *a* sound and the soft *g* sound. Read the word aloud.

4. Look at the pictures on page 6. Where do these animals live? What other animals would you find there?

Suggested levels for Guided Reading, DRA,™ Lexile,® and Reading Recovery™ are provided in the Pearson Scott Foresman Leveling Guide.

Social Studies

Genre	Comprehension Skills and Strategy
Nonfiction	• Cause and Effect • Author's Purpose • Monitor and Fix Up

Scott Foresman Reading Street 1.2.2

ISBN 0-328-13164-4

PEARSON
Scott Foresman
scottforesman.com

Social Studies

The Class

by Beatrice Reynolds

Many families have pets.
My family has a dog.
I like to walk our pup.

Many families like to have fun.
My family plays run and catch.
We like to laugh.

Many families shop together.

My family shops for food.

We put good things in bags.

No family is just like mine.

Is one of these families like yours?

Every effort has been made to secure permission and provide appropriate credit for photographic material. The publisher deeply regrets any omission and pledges to correct errors called to its attention in subsequent editions.

Unless otherwise acknowledged, all photographs are the property of Scott Foresman, a division of Pearson Education.

Photo locators denoted as follows: Top (T), Center (C), Bottom (B), Left (L), Right (R), Background (Bkgd)

Opener (C) Corbis; Opener (C) © Comstock Inc.; Opener (BL) Getty Images; 1 (C) Corbis; 1 (C) © Comstock Inc.; 1 (CL) Getty Images; 3 (B) Getty Images; 3 (T) © Comstock Inc.; 3 (T) Rubberball Productions; 3 (BC) © Comstock Inc.; 3 (BC) Rubberball Productions; 3 (CR) Rubberball Productions; 3 (CR) © Comstock Inc.; 4 (C) Stockbyte; 4 (C) © Comstock Inc.; 4 (BR) Corbis; 5 (BL) © Comstock Inc.; 5 (C) © Comstock Inc.; 5 (C) Digital Vision; 6 (C) Getty Images; 6 (C) © Comstock Inc.; 6 (BL) Brand X Pictures; 7 (BR) Getty Images; 7 (C) Getty Images; 7 (C) © Comstock Inc.; 8 (CR) Corbis; 8 (CR) © Comstock Inc.; 8 (TL) © Comstock Inc.; 8 (TL) Rubberball Productions; 8 (BL) © Comstock Inc.; 8 (BL) Corbis; 8 (BR) Brand X Pictures

ISBN: 0-328-13161-X

3 4 5 6 7 8 9 10 V010 14 13 12 11 10 09 08 07 06 05

Many families play games.
My family likes soccer.
I want to kick the ball.

No family is just like mine.

Is one of these families like yours?

All Kinds of Families

by Linda Yoshizawa

PEARSON
Scott Foresman

Editorial Offices: Glenview, Illinois • Parsippany, New Jersey • New York, New York
Sales Offices: Needham, Massachusetts • Duluth, Georgia • Glenview, Illinois
Coppell, Texas • Sacramento, California • Mesa, Arizona

Vocabulary

catch

good

no

put

want

Word count: 86

Note: The total word count includes words in the running text and headings only. Numerals and words in chapter titles, captions, labels, diagrams, charts, graphs, sidebars, and extra features are not included.

Think and Share

Read Together

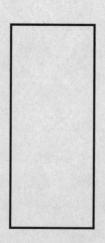

1. This book is about families. How are families in the book different? Name two ways.
2. Turn to page 6. The family is shopping. On your own paper, draw a box like this one. In it, draw a picture of what the family might do next.
3. Find the two words in the book that have the same vowel sound as the word *talk*.
4. Look at the picture of the boy on page 6. Tell what the family got at the store.

Suggested levels for Guided Reading, DRA™, Lexile,® and Reading Recovery™ are provided in the Pearson Scott Foresman Leveling Guide.

Social Studies

Genre	Comprehension Skills and Strategy
Nonfiction	• Main Idea • Compare and Contrast • Predict

Scott Foresman Reading Street 1.2.1

PEARSON
Scott Foresman
scottforesman.com

ISBN 0-328-13161-X

Social Studies

All Kinds of Families

by Linda Yoshizawa

We can see birds.

They live in a nest.

They are at home in the woods.

We can see a fox.

It can hunt in the snow.

It is at home in the woods.

We can see an ant.

It looks for its nest.

It is at home in the woods.

We hike into the woods.

Many animals live here.

Which animals will we see?

Every effort has been made to secure permission and provide appropriate credit for photographic material. The publisher deeply regrets any omission and pledges to correct errors called to its attention in subsequent editions.

Unless otherwise acknowledged, all photographs are the property of Scott Foresman, a division of Pearson Education.

Photo locators denoted as follows: Top (T), Center (C), Bottom (B), Left (L), Right (R), Background (Bkgd)

Opener Getty Images; 1 Digital Vision; 3 Getty Images; 4 Brand X Pictures; 5 Getty Images; 6 (B) © Kim Taylor/DK Images, 6 (T) Getty Images; 7 (BL) Getty Images, 7 (T) Digital Vision, 7 (C) Digital Vision; 8 DK Images

ISBN: 0-328-13158-X

3 4 5 6 7 8 9 10 V010 14 13 12 11 10 09 08 07 06 05

What a good hike in the woods!

We saw many animals at home

in the woods.

You can see them too!

Ants

Read Together

As we saw in the book, many different animals make their homes in the woods. Ants are one kind of woods animal. Ants live in nests that have many rooms and tunnels. The nests have one or more queen ants and lots of worker ants. The queen ant is the mother of all the ants in the nest. The worker ants take care of ant eggs and feed baby ants.

Will We See Animals?

by Megan Litwin

PEARSON
Scott Foresman

Editorial Offices: Glenview, Illinois • Parsippany, New Jersey • New York, New York
Sales Offices: Needham, Massachusetts • Duluth, Georgia • Glenview, Illinois
Coppell, Texas • Sacramento, California • Mesa, Arizona

Vocabulary

home

into

many

them

Word count: 86

Note: The total word count includes words in the running text and headings only. Numerals and words in chapter titles, captions, labels, diagrams, charts, graphs, sidebars, and extra features are not included.

Think and Share

Read Together

1. The family in the book saw animals. Why did they see animals?

What happened?
The family saw animals.

↓

Why did it happen?

2. Look at the picture of the fox on page 5. What does the picture show you about the weather in the woods?
3. Find and write the word from page 5 that has the short *u* sound and a final blend.
4. If you could ask an animal in this book a question, what would you ask about living in the woods?

Suggested levels for Guided Reading, DRA,™ Lexile,® and Reading Recovery™ are provided in the Pearson Scott Foresman Leveling Guide.

Genre	Comprehension Skills and Strategy
Realistic fiction	• Cause and Effect • Setting and Plot • Monitor and Fix Up

Scott Foresman Reading Street 1.1.6

PEARSON
Scott Foresman
scottforesman.com

ISBN 0-328-13158-X

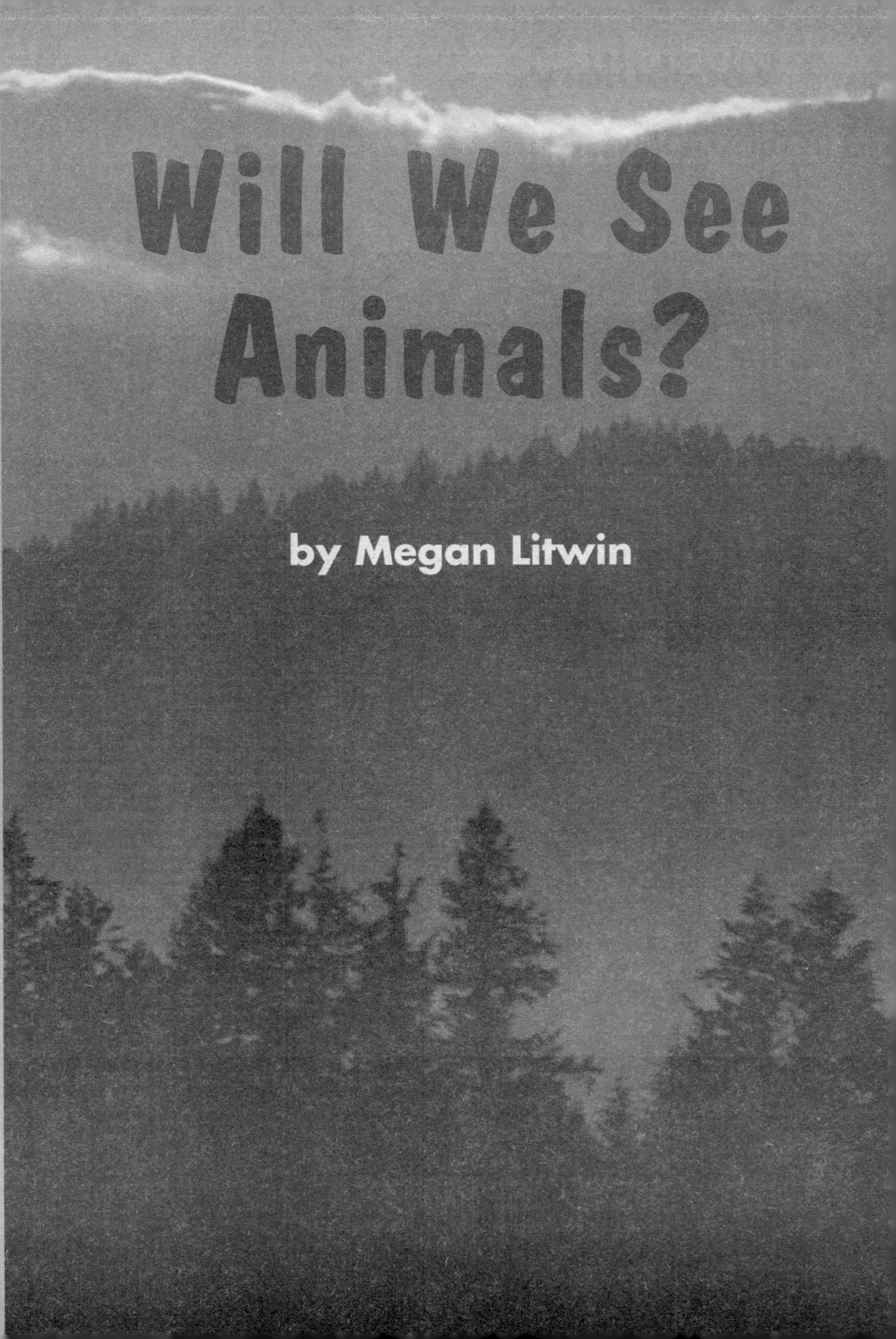

Will We See Animals?

by Megan Litwin

"Look in this log," said Dad.
"What do you see?"

"I can see a frog," said Fran.
"He is eating in this log."

"Look in this tree," said Mom.
"What do you see?"

"I can see small birds," said Fran.
"They are eating in the nest!"

"Look in the woods," said Mom.
"What do you see?"

"I can see a deer," said Fran.
"He is eating here."

Fran, Mom, and Dad went
for a walk.

"We can look for animals!"
said Fran.

Every effort has been made to secure permission and provide appropriate credit for photographic material. The publisher deeply regrets any omission and pledges to correct errors called to its attention in subsequent editions.

Unless otherwise acknowledged, all photographs are the property of Scott Foresman, a division of Pearson Education.

Photo locators denoted as follows: Top (T), Center (C), Bottom (B), Left (L), Right (R), Background (Bkgd)

Illustrations by Phyllis Polema Cahill

Photograph 8 (B) ©DK Images

ISBN: 0-328-13155-5

2 3 4 5 6 7 8 9 10 V010 14 13 12 11 10 09 08 07 06 05

"We saw animals eat dinner,"
said Fran.

"Do you want your dinner?"
said Dad.

"I do!" said Fran.

Birds in Nests

Read Together

Birds live in many different places. No matter where they live, most birds build nests. The mother bird lays her eggs in the nest. She sits on the eggs until they hatch. Then there are baby birds! Soon the baby birds grow up. When they grow up, they will leave the nest.

What Animals Do You See?

by Linda B. Ross
illustrated by Phyllis Polema Cahill

PEARSON Scott Foresman

Editorial Offices: Glenview, Illinois • Parsippany, New Jersey • New York, New York
Sales Offices: Needham, Massachusetts • Duluth, Georgia • Glenview, Illinois
Coppell, Texas • Ontario, California • Mesa, Arizona

Vocabulary

saw

small

tree

your

Word count: 100

Note: The total word count includes words in the running text and headings only. Numerals and words in chapter titles, captions, labels, diagrams, charts, graphs, sidebars, and extra features are not included.

Think and Share

Read Together

1. Could the kinds of animals in the book really live in the woods?

2. Copy the story chart on your own paper. Tell the characters, setting, and plot of *What Animals Do You See?*

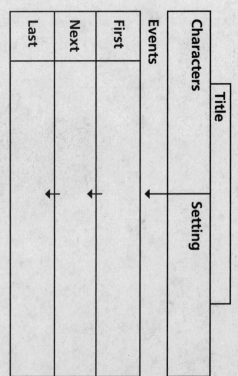

Title	
Characters	**Setting**

Events

First	
Next	
Last	

3. Point to the letters in the name *Fran*. Which letter is a vowel and which letters are consonants?

4. What other animals do you think Fran and her family could see on another walk?

Suggested levels for Guided Reading, DRA,™ Lexile,® and Reading Recovery™ are provided in the Pearson Scott Foresman Leveling Guide.

Genre	Comprehension Skills and Strategy
Realistic fiction	• Realism and Fantasy • Compare and Contrast • Story Structure

Scott Foresman Reading Street 1.1.5

ISBN 0-328-13155-5

PEARSON
Scott Foresman
scottforesman.com

What Animals Do You See?

by Linda B. Ross

illustrated by Phyllis Polema Cahill

This is a fox too.

She is in the zoo.

We like watching her.

She is looking back.

We see her sit.

This is a fox.

She is in the town.

She is looking for her dinner.

This is a fox.

She eats little animals.

She is in the woods.

Every effort has been made to secure permission and provide appropriate credit for photographic material. The publisher deeply regrets any omission and pledges to correct errors called to its attention in subsequent editions.

Unless otherwise acknowledged, all photographs are the property of Scott Foresman, a division of Pearson Education.

Illustrations by Wendy Rasmussen

ISBN: 0-328-13152-0

2 3 4 5 6 7 8 9 10 V010 14 13 12 11 10 09 08 07 06 05

This fox is in the zoo.

Sam has dinner for her.

We can watch her eat.

This is a fox.

That is a fox.

See where they live.

THIS FOX —AND— THAT FOX

BY LINDA LOTT

ILLUSTRATED BY WENDY RASMUSSEN

PEARSON Scott Foresman

Editorial Offices: Glenview, Illinois • Parsippany, New Jersey • New York, New York
Sales Offices: Needham, Massachusetts • Duluth, Georgia • Glenview, Illinois
Coppell, Texas • Ontario, California • Mesa, Arizona

Vocabulary

eat

her

this

too

Word count: 78

Note: The total word count includes words in the running text and headings only. Numerals and words in chapter titles, captions, labels, diagrams, charts, graphs, sidebars, and extra features are not included.

Think and Share

Read Together

1. What is *This Fox and That Fox* about?
2. What else would you like to know about foxes?
3. What does the letter *s* at the end of the word *animals* tell us about how many foxes we see in the story?
4. Look at the pictures on pages 6 and 7. Use a diagram like the one below to tell what is the same and what is different about how the foxes get their dinners.

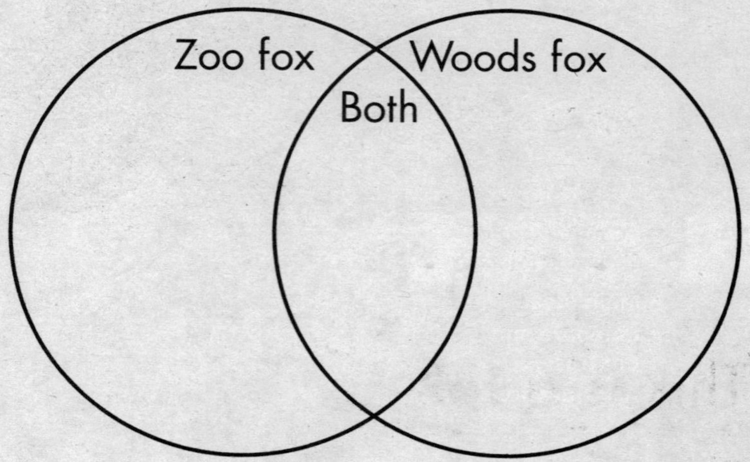

Suggested levels for Guided Reading, DRA,™ Lexile,® and Reading Recovery™ are provided in the Pearson Scott Foresman Leveling Guide.

Science

Genre	Comprehension Skills and Strategy
Realistic fiction	• Main Idea • Compare and Contrast • Ask Questions

Scott Foresman Reading Street 1.1.4

ISBN 0-328-13152-0
9 780328 131525 90000

PEARSON Scott Foresman
scottforesman.com

Science

Life Science

THIS FOX —AND— THAT FOX

BY LINDA LOTT

ILLUSTRATED BY WENDY RASMUSSEN

Tom and Tip are in the town.

Help!

Get us back to the farm!

Pam and Mops are in town.

They want to see the farm.

Pam and Mops are on the farm.

Help!

Get us back to town!

Tom and Tip are on the farm.

They want to see the town.

Every effort has been made to secure permission and provide appropriate credit for photographic material. The publisher deeply regrets any omission and pledges to correct errors called to its attention in subsequent editions.

Unless otherwise acknowledged, all photographs are the property of Scott Foresman, a division of Pearson Education.

Photo locators denoted as follows: Top (T), Center (C), Bottom (B), Left (L), Right (R), Background (Bkgd)

Illustrations by Bob Brugger

Photograph 8 ©DK Images

ISBN: 0-328-13149-0

3 4 5 6 7 8 9 10 V010 14 13 12 11 10 09 08 07 06 05

Tom and Tip use a tractor.

Pam and Mops use a cab.

They like where they are.

Where People Live

Read Together

People live in the city, in the country, in deserts, in the mountains, and in the jungle. People live all over the Earth! Some places have many people. Some places do not have many people.

Where do you live? Do many people live there?

Tom and Pam

by Kristin Cashore
illustrated by Bob Brugger

PEARSON
Scott Foresman

Editorial Offices: Glenview, Illinois • Parsippany, New Jersey • New York, New York
Sales Offices: Needham, Massachusetts • Duluth, Georgia • Glenview, Illinois
Coppell, Texas • Sacramento, California • Mesa, Arizona

Vocabulary

get

help

use

Word count: 69

Note: The total word count includes words in the running text and headings only. Numerals and words in chapter titles, captions, labels, diagrams, charts, graphs, sidebars, and extra features are not included.

Think and Share

Read Together

1. Who are the characters that like the farm? Draw the web on your own paper and write their names.

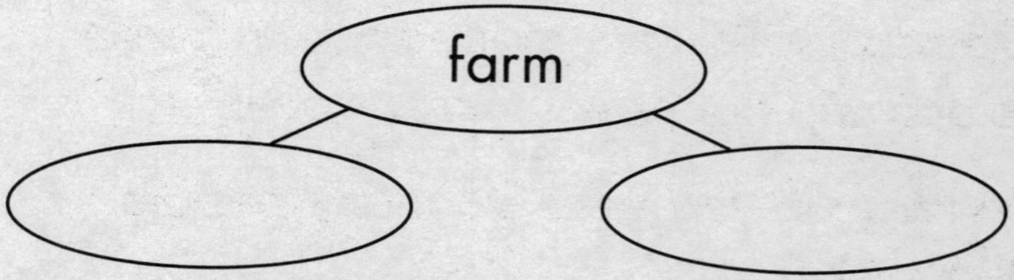

2. Picture Mops in your mind. How did he get his name?
3. Find the word *help* on pages 4 and 6. Why do the characters ask for help?
4. What do you think might happen if the characters spent more time in the kind of place they don't like?

Suggested levels for Guided Reading, DRA,™ Lexile,® and Reading Recovery™ are provided in the Pearson Scott Foresman Leveling Guide.

Genre	Comprehension Skills and Strategy
Realistic fiction	• Character and Setting • Theme and Plot • Visualize

Scott Foresman Reading Street 1.1.3

ISBN 0-328-13149-0
9 780328 131495 90000

PEARSON
Scott Foresman
scottforesman.com

Tom and Pam

by Kristin Cashore
illustrated by Bob Brugger

Here is Bix.
Bix is sick.

Here is Vin.
Vin is sick.

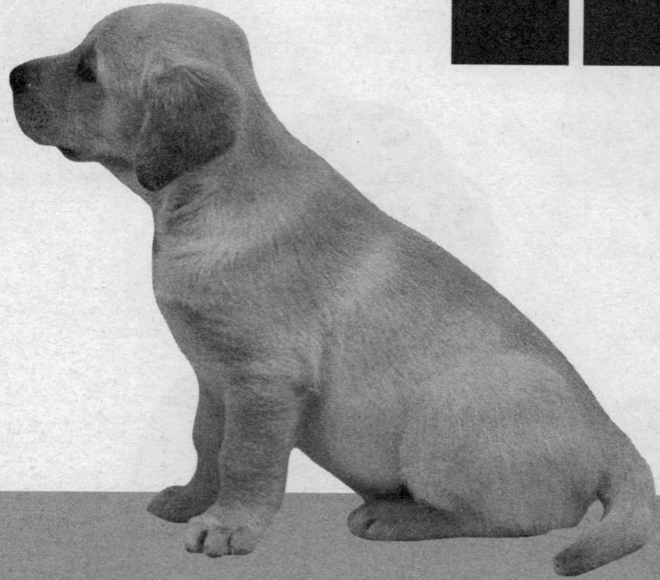

Here is the vet.
The vet can fix up Pip,
Bix, and Vin.

Here is Pip.
Pip is sick.

Every effort has been made to secure permission and provide appropriate credit for photographic material. The publisher deeply regrets any omission and pledges to correct errors called to its attention in subsequent editions.

Unless otherwise acknowledged, all photographs are the property of Scott Foresman, a division of Pearson Education.

Photo locators denoted as follows: Top (T), Center (C), Bottom (B), Left (L), Right (R), Background (Bkgd)

Opener © Comstock Inc.; 1 © Dorling Kindersley; 3 © Dorling Kindersley; 4 © Dorling Kindersley; 6 (TL) © Dorling Kindersley; 6 (B) © Dorling Kindersley; 7 © Dorling Kindersley; 8 © Comstock

ISBN: 0-328-13146-6

3 4 5 6 7 8 9 10 V010 14 13 12 11 10 09 08 07 06 05

Here is Tim.

Tim can take Vin back.

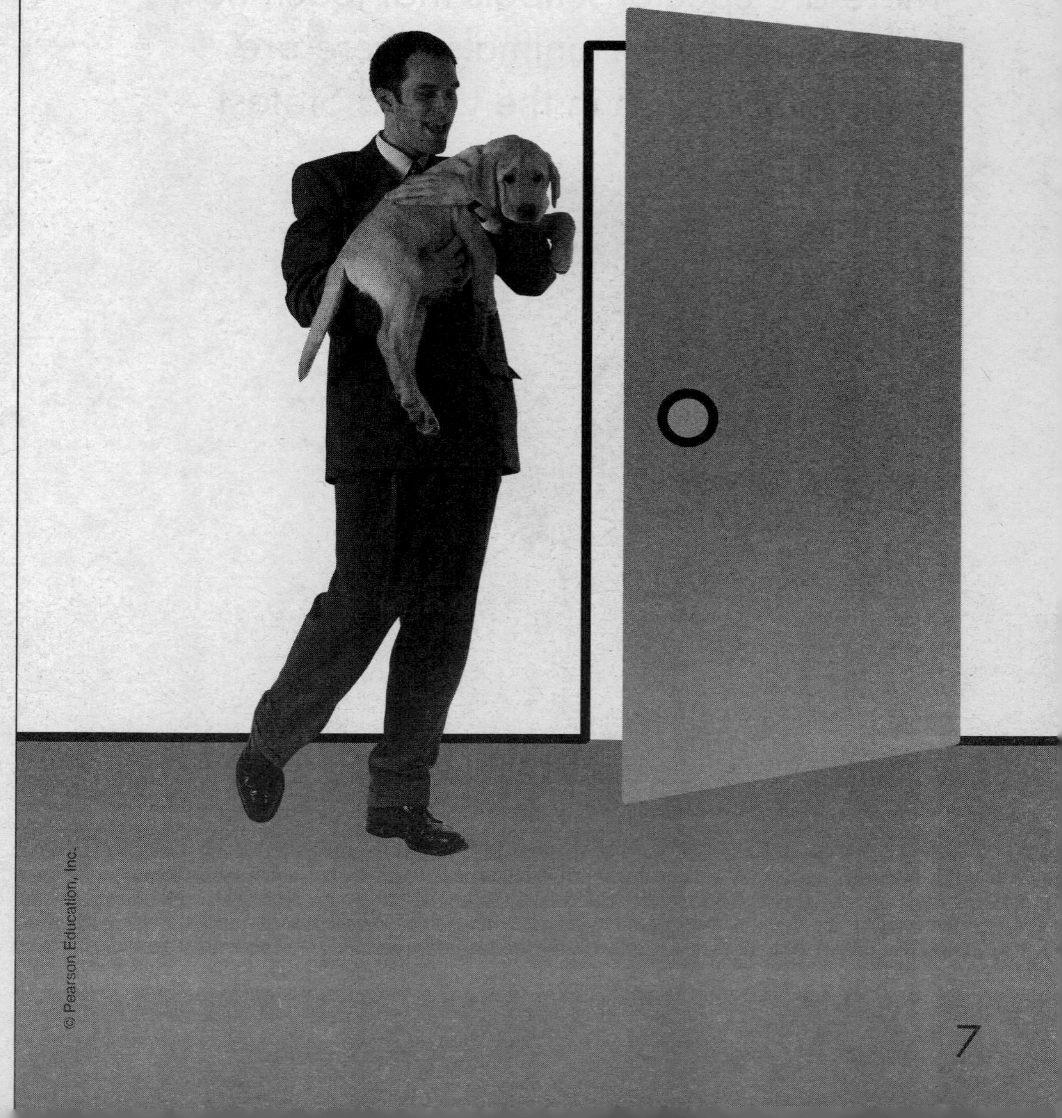

How to Be a Vet!

Read Together

Some people who like science and animals want to become vets. People go to school for many years to be vets. There are special schools that teach how to be a doctor for animals. There are thousands of vets in the United States!

They Are Sick

by Jessica Quilty

PEARSON Scott Foresman

Editorial Offices: Glenview, Illinois • Parsippany, New Jersey • New York, New York
Sales Offices: Needham, Massachusetts • Duluth, Georgia • Glenview, Illinois
Coppell, Texas • Sacramento, California • Mesa, Arizona

Vocabulary

and

take

up

Word count: 39

Note: The total word count includes words in the running text and headings only. Numerals and words in chapter titles, captions, labels, diagrams, charts, graphs, sidebars, and extra features are not included.

Think and Share

Read Together

1. Could a vet in real life see the kind of animal that is in this story?
2. What is the main thing you learned about vets from reading *They Are Sick*?
3. Find and write the two words in the story that have the sounds short *i* and final *x*. Use your own paper.

________	i	x
________	i	x

4. Vets can help heal sick pets. What would you ask a vet if you visited her office?

Suggested levels for Guided Reading, DRA™, Lexile,® and Reading Recovery™ are provided in the Pearson Scott Foresman Leveling Guide.

Genre	Comprehension Skills and Strategy
Realistic fiction	• Realism and Fantasy • Draw Conclusions • Summarize

Scott Foresman Reading Street 1.1.2

PEARSON
Scott Foresman
scottforesman.com

ISBN 0-328-13146-6
9 780328 131464 90000

They Are Sick

by Jessica Quilty

Can you see Mack the cat?
Mack can have a snack.

Can you see Mack the cat?
Mack can sleep on the mat.

Can you see Mack the cat?
Mack can see the way
to Zack.

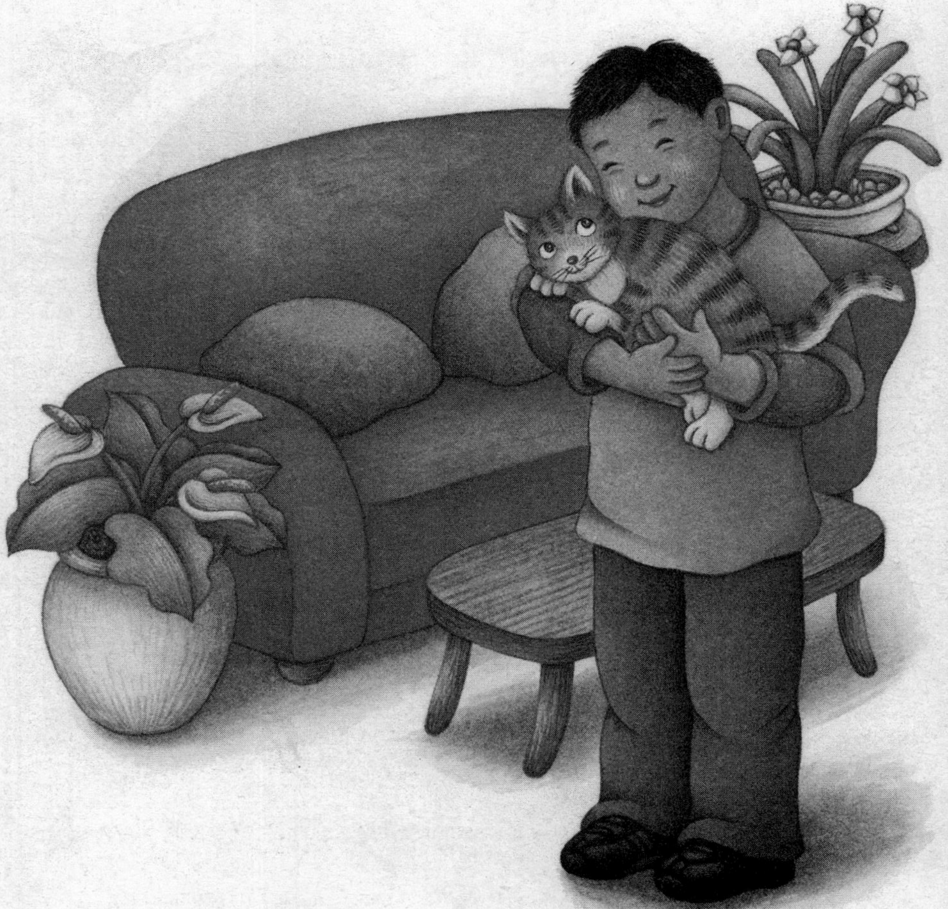

Can you see Mack the cat?
Mack can look at Zack.

Every effort has been made to secure permission and provide appropriate credit for photographic material. The publisher deeply regrets any omission and pledges to correct errors called to its attention in subsequent editions.

Unless otherwise acknowledged, all photographs are the property of Scott Foresman, a division of Pearson Education.

Photo locators denoted as follows: Top (T), Center (C), Bottom (B), Left (L), Right (R), Background (Bkgd)

Illustrations by Chi Chung

Photograph 8 ©Dorling Kindersley

ISBN: 0-328-13143-1

3 4 5 6 7 8 9 10 V010 14 13 12 11 10 09 08 07 06 05

Can you see Mack the cat?

Mack can nap in Zack's lap.

Caring for a Cat

Read Together

Cats need food and water each day. Someone should brush their fur. Brushing their fur helps cats stay clean. It is good for cats to play and nap. A cat can be a loving pet.

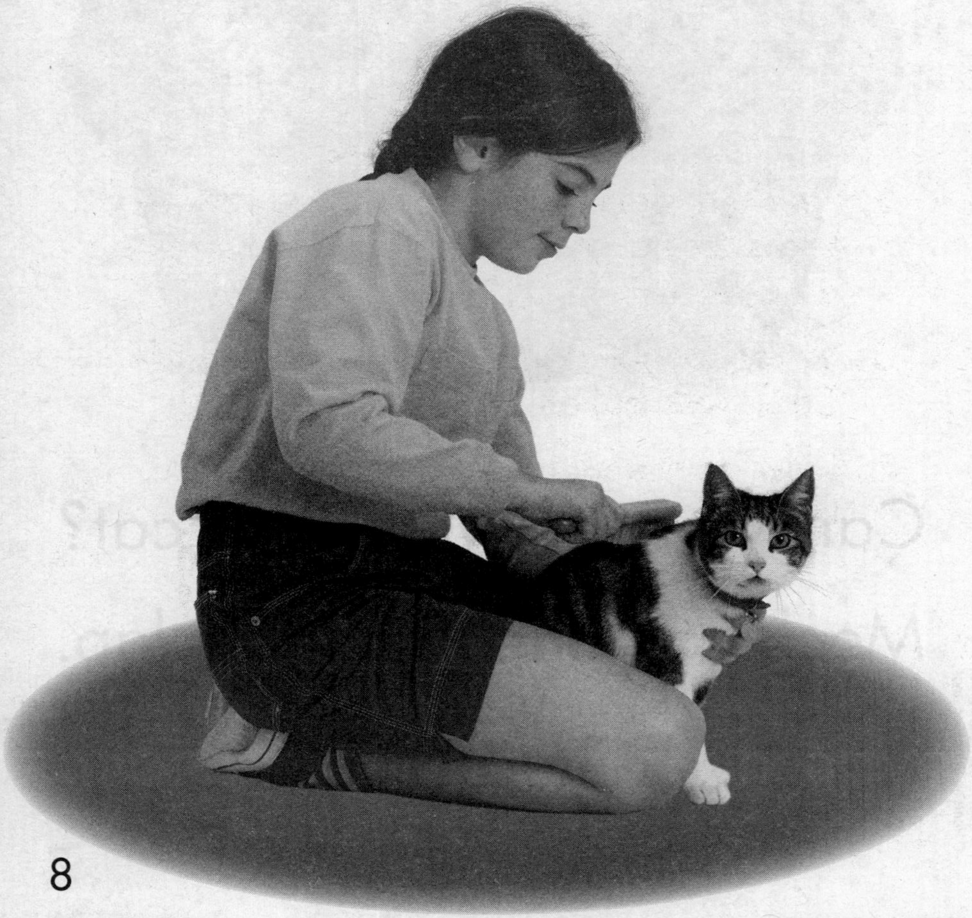

Mack the Cat

by Ann Rossi
illustrated by Chi Chung

PEARSON
Scott Foresman

Editorial Offices: Glenview, Illinois • Parsippany, New Jersey • New York, New York
Sales Offices: Needham, Massachusetts • Duluth, Georgia • Glenview, Illinois
Coppell, Texas • Sacramento, California • Mesa, Arizona